GOT QUESTIONS?
Got Answers

VOLUME TWO

Common Questions Asked by Christians and Religious People Every Day

Rich Kanyali

Unless otherwise noted, all scripture quotations are taken from the Holy Bible, King James Version. Public Domain.

Scripture quotations marked AMP are taken from the Amplified® Bible, Copyright © 1954, 1958, 1962, 1964, 1965, 1987 by The Lockman Foundation.

Used by permission.

Scripture quotations marked NIV are taken from the Holy Bible, New International Version®, NIV®. Copyright © 1973, 1978, 1984, 2011 by Biblica, Inc.™ Used by permission of Zondervan. All rights reserved worldwide.

www.zondervan.com The "NIV" and "New International Version" are trademarks registered in the United States Patent and Trademark Office by Biblica, Inc.™

Scripture quotations taken from The Message Bible are Copyright © 1993, 1994, 1995, 1996, 2000, 2001, 2002. Used by permission of NavPress Publishing Group.

Got Questions? Got Answers. (Volume II)

ISBN: 978-1-08801-676-3

Copyright © 2021 Rich Kanyali

All rights reserved. The text and cover graphic of this publication, or any part thereof, may not be reproduced in any manner whatsoever without written permission from the publisher.

Published by:

Rich Kanyali

RichKanyali.com

RichKanyaliBooks@outlook.com

info@RichKanyali.com

Table of Contents

Acknowledgments and Special Thanks   5

Introduction   7

Chapter One
Is God sovereign?   9

Chapter Two
What is Universal salvation? Are all men saved and just don't know it? Has everyone been reconciled to God? What difference does it make for one to believe?   19

Chapter Three
Can a Christian "lose" his salvation or depart from the faith?   33

Chapter Four
Why live a godly life? Are there any benefits of living a godly life?   45

Chapter Five
What about tithes and offerings?   57

Chapter Six
How can I know God's will?   71

Chapter Seven
What about healing?   79

Chapter Eight
I thought I was healed, but I'm sick again. What happened to my healing?   87

Chapter Nine
Is it God's will to heal me?   97

Chapter Ten
What does God hate?   105

Chapter Eleven
How is Christianity different from all the other religions?   121

Chapter Twelve
What is the fear of the Lord?   141

Chapter Thirteen
Does God use or send problems to teach and perfect us?   163

Chapter Fourteen
What is free will?   181

Chapter Fifteen
Is Hell a reality, a myth or a metaphor?   187

Chapter Sixteen
Why do I have to go to church if God is everywhere?   193

Receive Jesus As Your Savior   199

Receive the Baptism of the Holy Spirit   200

Acknowledgments and Special Thanks

I would like to give special thanks to the following people who have made and continue to make a major positive impact on my life:

Jesus Christ–Lord, You are my personal Lord and Savior. You have been my Guide and Teacher. Lord, I thank You for changing my life and blessing me beyond measure. I adore You and I'm forever grateful for Your finished work on the cross. Thank You so much for Your unconditional and infinite love for me. Thank You for the increased and supernatural revelation You have given me through Your Word and the anointing to communicate it with simplicity and clarity. I trust, and totally depend on, You. Thank you for the lives you are going to speak to and touch through this book. I give You all the glory and honor, the Lover of my soul. Thank You, Lord Jesus.

Andrew Wommack (President and Founder of Andrew Wommack Ministries and Charis Bible College)–It's an absolute privilege and an honor to serve at your ministry. I have learned a lot from you over the past many years. You have taught and inspired me so much. Your humility is very admirable. Things I have learned from you have guided and transformed my life and have birthed many books that I have written and will write. Thank you so very much.

Pastor Greg Mohr (Former Director of Charis Bible College)–Pastor Greg, you are a man of wisdom and humility. You have taught me so much. Thank you for pouring out your heart to help grow, change, and impact my life. I'm forever grateful.

Introduction

I have had a heart to help answer people's questions since childhood. When I was born again, I had so many questions. The Lord has answered many of them over the years. This desire to answer questions later led me to Charis Bible College for ministry training where I graduated with a Masters in Biblical Studies and now serve as the Director of Andrew Wommack Ministries and Charis Bible College, Uganda.

Although, I have a heart to answer questions, I realize that not every question people ask must be addressed. People have different reasons for asking questions that no one can fully address or even get into. Not all questions people ask have the same motive of knowing the truth. Some questions are to debate, cast more doubt, or argue. We must learn to discern the spirit behind the question. Some questions have a preconceived notion, others are accusatory, others are assumptive, while other questions may only be a trap. Not all questions are created equal, nor in the same image. Therefore, not all questions need to be answered.

"But foolish and unlearned questions avoid, knowing that they do gender strifes."
– 2 Timothy 2:23

I must confess that none of us has all the answers. That's why we need to learn to walk by faith. The Word of God clearly teaches that, in this life, we know in part (1 Corinthians 13:12). Yet, I believe that *part* that we do know is big enough for us to live a victorious Christian life. For all the answers that we genuinely need to know, the Lord has already provided in the Bible.

If you have questions that have not been answered yet, stick to what you already know and do not throw away what you do know because of what you do not know.

With discipleship and teaching in mind, I will be shooting straight with an in-depth Bible study approach in the attempt to answer these questions as quickly and directly as possible. This way, I can answer the question and at the

GOT QUESTIONS?

same time impart some guidance, teaching, reproof, and instruction to build you up. I believe in the infallibility of the Word of God; therefore, all my answers will be derived from the Holy Bible and the revelation that God has given me—some directly and some through other people. I believe there is no better source of answers than the Word of God; therefore, I will stick with what it teaches. Asking and answering questions is a huge foundation for learning, for the one asking and the one being asked.

Buckle up, buckle in and let's roll.

Chapter One

Is God Sovereign?

Whenever people don't understand why they are going through pain, chaos or hardship, they usually say: "nothing happens but what God allows", "God is sovereign; therefore, His will shall always come to pass no matter what, because He controls everything." Nothing could be further from the truth.

Our lack of understanding should not result in slandering and blaming God as the One who is sovereign and therefore in control of everything that happens in our lives. Although, this may bring temporary relief to suffering people, it is at the expense of God's integrity and loving nature. It slanders God and holds Him responsible for everything that happens. How wrong this is!

The word "sovereign" doesn't exist anywhere in the King James Bible. It is used in the NIV over 300 times, but even then, it is not used the way religious people have taken it to mean. Religious people say God is sovereign, above all in power and authority; therefore, He controls everything that happens. This is simply not true.

a) God is sovereign, if that word is used as the dictionary defines it, not as the religious people use it. The word *"sovereign"* means *supreme, paramount, above all in power and authority*. The doctrine of God's sovereignty, meaning "in control of everything" has brought great damage to the church.

GOT QUESTIONS?

    i) It's the greatest faith-killer and opens the door for Satan to come in and steal, kill and destroy.

    ii) It renders people inactive and extremely passive. They develop the mentality of "whatever will be, will be." Oh, how I hate that thinking!

    iii) What's the point of doing anything if God controls everything?

- Why believe?
- Why give?
- Why seek God?
- Why get saved?
- Why love people?
- Why do anything if God ultimately controls everything?

b) If that's true, then it makes no sense for God to instruct or command us to do anything because "He ultimately controls everything." Do you see something desperately wrong with that thinking? I do. This thinking has doomed many because the assumption is that one doesn't have to believe on Jesus as Lord and Savior because nothing happens unless God controls it, allows it and is responsible for everything that happens.

God, in His sovereignty, limited Himself. God is sovereign in the bounds that He can do anything within His own will, character, nature, and Word. There are some things He cannot do. He cannot break His Word, He cannot lie, and He cannot sin.

Some say God always gets what He wants and whenever He wants. Even God does not always get what He wants. God in His sovereignty chose to limit Himself by giving us a freewill. The Word of God teaches that God doesn't always get what He wants (2 Peter 3:9; 1 Timothy 2:4). These verses show that man does have a freewill and he exercises it as well (Deuteronomy 30:19; Joshua 24:15, 22; Judges 10:14).

Chapter One

Did you know that love is not love once it has no free will? Forcing yourself on someone else or demanding that they love you is not love. Genuine love has free will. Did you know that when you get married, you keep your freewill? This is also true when someone is born again.

God does not make decisions for you. You have a free will and it comes with responsibility.

There are two main things I have learned about sovereignty:

a) God is the owner or has ownership

   Ownership doesn't necessarily mean control. You can own something, yet delegate control and rulership to someone else. Many people mistake ownership for control, rulership and stewardship. God chose to delegate the rulership, stewardship, and dominion of the earth to man.

   i) *"For the earth is the Lord's, and the fulness thereof."* –1 Corinthians 10:26

   ii) *"The earth is the LORD's, and the fulness thereof; the world, and they that dwell therein."* –Psalm 24:1

   iii) *"If I were hungry, I would not tell thee: for the world is mine, and the fulness thereof."* –Psalm 50:12

   iv) *"The heavens are thine, the earth also is thine: as for the world and the fullness thereof, thou hast founded them."* –Psalm 89:11

b) Man is the steward or has rulership

   Although God has the ownership, He delegated stewardship, dominion, and rulership to man. Because of this, many bad things happen because of the one in stewardship and rulership but not because of the owner, God. **Simply put, God allows what we allow.** This is how God works together with man here on earth–through dominion and stewardship. Man has the lease of the earth until the return of the Lord.

GOT QUESTIONS?

As an example, I currently as Director of Andrew Wommack Ministries Uganda make certain decisions as steward and as one who has responsibility, yet it is not Andrew Wommack who made them.

He delegated authority to me which came with responsibility. He should not be the one to blame if I were to make bad decisions as one who has been entrusted as a steward.

i) *"And God said, Let us make man in our image, after our likeness: and let them have dominion over the fish of the sea, and over the fowl of the air, and over the cattle, and over all the earth, and over every creeping thing that creepeth upon the earth. So God created man in his own image, in the image of God created he him; male and female created he them. And God blessed them, and God said unto them, Be fruitful, and multiply, and replenish the earth, and subdue it: and have dominion over the fish of the sea, and over the fowl of the air, and over every living thing that moveth upon the earth."* –Genesis 1:26-28

ii) *"Thou madest him to have dominion over the works of thy hands; thou hast put all things under his feet."* –Psalm 8:6

iii) *"The heaven, even the heavens, are the L*ORD*'s: but the earth hath he given to the children of men."* –Psalm 115:16

God gave these to His body:

- Authority and power over all the power of the enemy
- Name of Jesus
- The Holy Spirit living on the inside of us.
- Faith of God
- Power to bind and loose
- Better covenant established on better promises
- Commission to do greater works than Jesus
- His written Word

If God is truly in control, or is controlling, all of the events on earth, why did He give His church the above tools to destroy the works of the

Chapter One

devil? (1 John 3:8). The Church has a major part to play because of the delegated authority God has given her. We have been heavily equipped for success–glory to God!

"The Lord is not slack concerning his promise, as some men count slackness; but is longsuffering to us-ward, not willing that any should perish, but that all should come to repentance."

–2 Peter 3:9

i) *"Enter ye in at the strait gate: for wide is the gate, and broad is the way, that leadeth to destruction, and many there be which go in thereat: Because strait is the gate, and narrow is the way, which leadeth unto life, and few there be that find it."* –Matthew 7:13-14

ii) Look at the two verses above. One verse (2 Peter 3:9) says God wills none to perish but repent, while the other (Matthew 7:13-14) says they are perishing and heading full speed to hell. Why is it so, if God controls and is responsible for everything? This is because God doesn't control everything. People have a choice on how they want their life to play out.

"I call heaven and earth to record this day against you, that I have set before you life and death, blessing and cursing: therefore choose life, that both thou and thy seed may live:"

–Deuteronomy 30:19

i) In this verse, we see God giving us a free will or right to choose what we want, but He went ahead and gave us good guidance on how to choose. He says to choose life.

ii) Notice, you have to choose. He doesn't choose for you.

- With choice comes responsibility.

iii) God is not responsible for everything that happens in our lives because we get to choose.

GOT QUESTIONS?

- For God to be responsible for all our choices or things we go through, He has to be the one choosing for us.

iv) Each of us has a free will to choose. For that reason, things happen that are not God's fault. He doesn't make us or force us to choose; people go to hell because they choose it. It's their own choice that sends them into eternal damnation.

v) It's not God who is responsible, controls, and ordains everything. Many things that happen to us are as a result of our choices, which cause problems and disorder, in addition to attacks of Satan.

vi) We have a whole lot of responsibility laid at our feet. We can't just shrug it off and say God is responsible because He is sovereign. We must take responsibility lest we perish.

"Submit yourselves therefore to God. Resist the devil, and he will flee from you."
—James 4:7

i) Notice that this verse tells us to *"resist"* the devil. This verse gives us the responsibility to do so.

ii) If God is sovereign in the sense that He controls everything and is responsible for all that happens, why does His Word tell us to resist the devil? Why resist if God controls everything?

iii) The word *"resist"* is not a passive word, but an active word. It's saying that we must actively fight against the devil.

"And he could there do no mighty work, save that he laid his hands upon a few sick folk, and healed them. And he marveled because of their unbelief. And he went round about the villages, teaching."
—Mark 6:5-6

i) Notice that this verse says He <u>could</u> not do, not He <u>would</u> not do.

Chapter One

    ii) God was willing, but the unbelief of the people hindered Him from healing them.

        ◦ If God controls everything and is sovereign, why couldn't He heal them all?

    iii) Think about this: If God was responsible for everything and controlled it all, then why didn't these people receive their miracles? It's simple. It's because they had a part to play in this and God couldn't do it for them.

"Blessed is the man that endureth temptation: for when he is tried, he shall receive the crown of life, which the Lord hath promised to them that love him. Let no man say when he is tempted, I am tempted of God: for God cannot be tempted with evil, neither tempteth he any man: But every man is tempted, when he is drawn away of his own lust, and enticed. Then when lust hath conceived, it bringeth forth sin: and sin, when it is finished, bringeth forth death. Do not err, my beloved brethren. **Every good gift and every perfect gift is from above, and cometh down from the Father of lights, with whom is no variableness, neither shadow of turning."** (emphasis mine)

–James 1:12-17

    i) Because of the unbiblical doctrine of sovereignty, people believe that God is responsible for all the bad and evil things. They believe that since He is sovereign, He can stop everything and He controls it all. The verses concerning man's free will dismantle the belief that God controls everything, or that He is responsible for everything.

    ii) James 1:12-17 tells us that it is good that comes from God. It does not say evil comes from Him.

    iii) God tempts no man. Man is tempted by his own lust.

        ◦ If God controls everything or is sovereign then He is responsible for every bad thing as well?

GOT QUESTIONS?

iv) What comes from God is good and perfect gifts, not evil. These verses should settle that. God is not responsible for the bad things and evil in our lives.

v) Death, sickness, divorce, calamity, suffering, poverty, destruction, loss, brokenness, misery; all these are neither good nor perfect gifts. No one would wrap these as birthday or Christmas gifts for someone else as a blessing.

"How God anointed Jesus of Nazareth with the Holy Ghost and with power: who went about doing good, and healing all that were oppressed of the devil; for God was with him."

–Acts 10:38

i) The teaching of sovereignty says that sickness and oppression are from God and He allows, controls and is responsible for it.

ii) That kind of thinking makes Satan look good and makes God the bad guy. However, this Scripture among many others clearly says the very opposite.

iii) Those who were sick were oppressed of the devil, not of God. There is a devil out there and he is responsible for all the evil.

iv) Jesus was healing those that the devil was busy oppressing. So, God is not responsible for the evil that happens. He was about good.

v) He is good and goodness is His nature.

"The thief cometh not, but for to steal, and to kill, and to destroy: I am come that they might have life, and that they might have it more abundantly."

–John 10:10

i) If God controls and is responsible for everything, then why does this verse say that Satan comes to steal, kill, and destroy while God brings abundant life.

Chapter One

ii) God is not the One responsible for the bad things that happen to you. Neither is He the One who controls nor allows it. God is a good God and the devil is a bad devil all the time.

iii) God is the answer to all our problems, while Satan, our choices, and the imperfect world we live in are the causes of our problems, not God. It's so simple.

Let me end with this thought that God gave me years ago while I was studying and thinking about this subject. In the word "good" you find the word God and in the word "devil", you find the word evil.

Chapter Two

What is Universal Salvation? Are all men saved and just don't know it? Have all been reconciled to God? What difference does it make for one to believe?

Some in the grace circle believe that all people are already born again (saved) and they just need to be made aware of this, that they are already in Christ. Along the same lines, others believe that there is no hell. These are simply false doctrines and do not reflect the teaching of the Word.

We have a responsibility to believe. We are not born again by default. We are saved by God's grace, but we need to exercise faith into that grace (Ephesians 2:8-9).

Many who believe such have overemphasized certain words to the exclusion of the whole Word of God. These people use verses like 1 Corinthians 15:22: "For as in Adam all die, even so in Christ shall all be made alive". Some have taken this verse to mean that since all were subject to death in Adam, all are made alive in Jesus, and that we do not have to believe in the Lord because we are already **in** Christ. It is also not speaking of being saved. This is saying that only those who are IN Christ through faith (Ephesians 2:8-9) shall all be made alive. No one is made alive in Jesus outside of faith.

Those who have chosen to believe that all men are saved have ignored hundreds of verses that clearly teach that we need to believe in Jesus to be saved. Others have believed that there will be a reconciliation after a period of time, but that is not accurate either. If it were, why do we have to believe? Why did Jesus come? Why did Jesus have to come and die on the cross for our sins? There is no Scripture in the Word of God that takes away our responsibility to believe. Those who do not believe will be eternally doomed and separated from God.

- a) *"For the preaching of the cross is to them that perish foolishness; but unto us which are saved it is the power of God."* –I Corinthians 1:18

    - i) Notice that some are saved while others are perishing or perish. If all be saved, the Lord would never have said this.

- b) *"For after that in the wisdom of God the world by wisdom knew not God, it pleased God by the foolishness of preaching to save them that believe. "* –1 Corinthians 1:21

    - i) Notice the words "preaching to save those who believe." This is speaking of the preaching of the Gospel through which people are saved through faith. Preaching is being done, but people MUST believe to be saved.

- c) *"I said therefore unto you, that ye shall die in your sins: for if ye believe not that I am he, ye shall die in your sins."* –John 8:24

    - i) Jesus told us how to come alive in Him. It is by and through faith.

    - ii) Those who die in their sins will eternally be separated from God and this is because they believed not that Jesus died for the sins and rose from the dead.

- d) *"For God so loved the world, that he gave his only begotten Son, that whosoever believeth in him should not perish, but have everlasting life."* – John 3:16

    - i) This verse says whosoever believeth in Him should not perish. People have a choice to believe or not, hence the term "whosoever."

    - ii) Some will perish, some will not. The difference is down to those believing.

iii) God's love is evident and not in question for those who want to see it; however, those who do not believe, Jesus said they will perish. This is the truth. Those that say otherwise are either lying, ignorant or deceived.

e) *"Go ye therefore, and teach all nations, baptizing them in the name of the Father, and of the Son, and of the Holy Ghost:"* –Matthew 28:19

   i) Why did Jesus give us the Great Commission if all have been saved?

   ii) Why should the Gospel be preached in all the world and why should all men repent if all men are born again and are already reconciled to God?

   - *"And saying, The time is fulfilled, and the kingdom of God is at hand: repent ye and believe the Gospel."* –Mark 1:15

   - *"And the times of this ignorance God winked at; but now commandeth all men every where to repent:"* –Acts 17:30

f) *"To wit, that God was in Christ, reconciling the world unto himself, not imputing their trespasses unto them; and hath committed unto us the word of reconciliation. Now then we are ambassadors for Christ, as though God did beseech you by us: we pray you in Christ's stead, be ye reconciled to God."* –2 Corinthians 5:19-20

   i) There are two sides to this reconciliation. God was in Christ reconciling the world to Himself, which is true, but the next verse tells us of the other side of reconciliation.

   ii) Man must be reconciled to God. Man has a part to play and that part is the faith part. Man must believe or else he will not be reconciled to God.

   iii) If we are already reconciled to God, why would we be told to *"be reconciled."*

iv) Some have argued that we have already been reconciled but need to preach the Gospel only because people need Jesus now, in this life, because of the sufferings and hardships we go through, but they forget that the hardship and the torment of hell and the lake of fire is infinitely greater than the struggles of this world. If we need Jesus for the insignificant struggles of this world as they pontificate, then we definitely need Him even more to free us from the eternal hardships of hell. If we need Jesus for life insurance, we need Him for fire insurance at the least.

g) *"To the weak became I as weak, that I might gain the weak: I am made all things to all men, that I might by all means save some."* – 1 Corinthians 9:22

i) Paul was saying that he chose to be all things to all men for the purpose of saving some. Notice that this verse says, "save some", not all. Paul had a heart to reach people at all cost but recognized that he could not save all. They had to believe, which some would not do.

ii) People have free will. They can choose to believe in the Lord Jesus or not. Those who believe will be saved, but those who do not will not "be saved."

h) *"And with all deceivableness of unrighteousness in them that perish; because they received not the love of the truth, that they might be saved."* –2 Thessalonians 2:10

i) It is not automatic that all people are saved. Jesus has paid and died for their sins, but they must believe and receive. Salvation is a gift, but it must be received through faith. We have a part to play.

Believe to be saved

All people are not born again (in relationship, reconciled with God eternally in heaven). Each of us must believe to be born again (born of God) and enter into a personal relationship with God through the Lord Jesus Christ. We must believe

Chapter Two

that when we die we will spend eternity with the Lord, not apart from Him. This happens when we accept Jesus Christ in our hearts as our Lord and Savior, believing that He died on the cross for our sins and rose again from the dead.

a) *"For if Abraham were justified by works, he hath whereof to glory; but not before God. For what saith the scripture? Abraham believed God, and it was counted unto him for righteousness. Now to him that worketh is the reward not reckoned of grace, but of debt. But to him that worketh not, but believeth on him that justifieth the ungodly, his faith is counted for righteousness."* –Romans 4:2-5

　　i) Abraham believed God and was declared righteous.

　　ii) To be justified, to be made righteous with God, to be born again, and to come into relationship with God through Jesus, you must only believe.

b) *"But as many as received him, to them gave he power to become the sons of God, even to them that believe on his name:"* –John 1:12

　　i) All who believe, or believed, in Christ Jesus have been given the power to become the sons of God. I have spoken to many folks people who claim to be children of God yet they have not believed in Jesus.

　　　　○ Unbelievers are not sons nor children of God. Children, or sons, of God are those who have put faith in Jesus. Many think that all people are children of God, but that is not true. All people are a creation of God, but they are not children until they believe in Him. Huge difference.

　　ii) Notice it says "those who believe" which indicates that some might not. Two, it makes clear that they must believe.

c) *"For God so loved the world, that he gave his only begotten Son, that whosoever believeth in him should not perish, but have everlasting life."* –John 3:16

- i) This promise is to those who believe; salvation comes by believing.
- ii) We are saved (born again) through faith in Jesus, not through our works or performance (Titus 3:5). Circumcision, water baptism, tithing, giving alms, going to church, etc. do not produce salvation.
- iii) We MUST believe in the Lord Jesus Christ to be saved.

d) *"He that believeth on the Son hath everlasting life: and he that believeth not the Son shall not see life; but the wrath of God abideth on him."* –John 3:36

- i) He that believes in the Son (Jesus) has everlasting life.
  - It does **not** say that all men believe and have everlasting life.
  - It takes only **believing** to be born again hence entering into relationship with God (everlasting life).
- ii) Not seeing life means they will see death and the wrath of God (i.e. hell).

e) *"Then said they unto him, What shall we do, that we might work the works of God? Jesus answered and said unto them, This is the work of God, that ye believe on him whom he hath sent."* –John 6:28-29

- i) These men sincerely wanted to know what they could DO to be saved. This verse revealed to them what they had to DO. It was to believe on Him. That's the work that one MUST do.
- ii) According to Colossians 2:6, we received Jesus by faith and we continue to walk with Him and receive from Him by faith.

f) *"But these are written, that ye might believe that Jesus is the Christ, the Son of God; and that believing ye might have life through his name."* –John 20:31

- i) Believing in Jesus produces life.

g) *"Neither is there salvation in any other: for there is none other name under heaven given among men, whereby we must be saved."* –Acts 4:12

Chapter Two

- i) Salvation comes only by faith in the name of Jesus, not in the name of Buddha, Krishna, Mohammed, and so forth.

h) *"Therefore by the deeds of the law there shall no flesh be justified in his sight: for by the law is the knowledge of sin. But now the righteousness of God without the law is manifested, being witnessed by the law and the prophets; Even the righteousness of God which is by faith of Jesus Christ unto all and upon all them that believe: for there is no difference: For all have sinned, and come short of the glory of God; Being justified freely by his grace through the redemption that is in Christ Jesus: Whom God hath set forth to be a propitiation through faith in his blood, to declare his righteousness for the remission of sins that are past, through the forbearance of God; To declare, I say, at this time his righteousness: that he might be just, and the justifier of him which believeth in Jesus."* –Romans 3:20-26

  - i) There is no good act or work that can make any man righteous before God. If our performance could justify us, there would be no need for Jesus. Jesus came because our deeds, actions, and performances could not produce the righteousness of God.

  - ii) The righteousness of God comes by faith in and of Jesus to all that believe.

i) *"Therefore being justified by faith, we have peace with God through our Lord Jesus Christ:"* –Romans 5:1

  - i) We are justified by faith–not by the law, works, or performance.

j) *"That if thou shalt confess with thy mouth the Lord Jesus, and shalt believe in thine heart that God hath raised him from the dead, thou shalt be saved. For with the heart man believeth unto righteousness; and with the mouth confession is made unto salvation."* –Romans 10:9-10

  - i) Notice this says to believe (not work or perform) in your heart that God raised Jesus from the dead, then you shall be saved. You have to do the believing to be saved–believe that God raised Jesus from the dead.

k) *"But the scripture hath concluded all under sin, that the promise by faith of Jesus Christ might be given to them that believe; For ye are all the children of God by faith in Christ Jesus."* –Galatians 3:22,26

   i) The promise is for those who believe, not for those who work.

   ii) We become children of God by faith in the Lord Jesus Christ.

l) *"For by grace are ye saved through faith; and that not of yourselves: it is the gift of God: Not of works, lest any man should boast."* –Ephesians 2:8-9

   i) We are born again (saved) by grace through faith. We put faith in God's grace (Jesus and His finished work on the cross).

m) *"And brought them out, and said, Sirs, what must I do to be saved? And they said, Believe on the Lord Jesus Christ, and thou shalt be saved, and thy house. And they spake unto him the word of the Lord, and to all that were in his house."* –Acts 16:30-32

   i) When these men asked how to be saved, Paul gave them an answer that further verifies what I have been saying in this teaching. He did not say, "You are already born again (saved) and reconciled to God". He said, "Believe on the Lord Jesus Christ and thou shalt be saved." Period.

n) *"But for us also, to whom it shall be imputed, if we believe on him that raised up Jesus our Lord from the dead;"* –Romans 4:24.

   i) God does not issue salvation. Salvation is a gift. If salvation were issued, then faith would not be required. It is a gift because we have a choice to receive it or reject it. People MUST believe on Him who raised Jesus from the dead. If we do not believe that Jesus was raised from the dead, then righteousness and right standing with God cannot be imputed to us.

Universalism beliefs violate these three things among many others:

Chapter Two

i) Free will of man as explained ealier

ii) Authority of man

- God gave man authority and with this authority comes responsibility. He does not exercise that authority for us. We do that ourselves.

iii) Love of God

- God would not force His love on one who does not want it. God's kind of love is not forceful. When you love a person, you let them choose. A freewill is foundational to love.

Four things you must believe to be born again

I met a young muslim lady who tried to convince me of her love for Jesus, but she had never believed on Him. I told her that to love Jesus is to accept or believe on Him in her heart as Lord and Savior.

Many people use a wrong acid test as to whether a person is born again or not. They use actions and morality as a sign that someone is born again. Good morals do not fully depict believing. Some unbelievers are moral people, but that does not make them born again.

According to the Scriptures, true salvation is not determined by good deeds or how moral a person is, but by what they believe. What a person believes is the true test of someone being truly born again.

We are born again by what we believe, not by what we do. This is not to say our actions are not important; they are. However, the Scripture bases salvation on believing, not on performance, This is a striking truth that many have missed.

Many people say they believe in God. With this, I presume they are referring to God the Father, not Jesus. However, to truly believe in God, we do that by believing in Jesus. Those who have not believed in Jesus do not truly believe in God.

GOT QUESTIONS?

Jesus is The Way (John 14:6-7) and The Door (John 10:7-9) to believing in God. In other words, you must believe in Jesus first to believe in God the Father. Any other means are invalid. It disqualifies us; furthermore, the only acceptable and valid means of the entrance into relationship with God and His family (sheepfold) is through the door (Jesus). Anyone who attempts to use any other means such as a window (any other means and religion) as the entrance and not the door is a thief and robber (John 10:1-10).

It is after we believe in Jesus that we believe in God the Father and the Holy Spirit. It's like a sale where they say, "buy one, get one free or in some cases get two free (You do not get two free until you buy one). This "One" is Jesus and the currency you use is faith. When you believe in Jesus, you get both the Father and Holy Spirit.

For a person to be truly born again, he or she must meet the requirements of the Scriptures as detailed by Paul in the passage below.

"Moreover, brethren, I declare unto you the Gospel which I preached unto you, which also ye have received, and wherein ye stand; By which also ye are saved, if ye keep in memory what I preached unto you, unless ye have believed in vain. For I delivered unto you first of all that which I also received, how that Christ died for our sins according to the scriptures; And that he was buried, and that he rose again the third day according to the scriptures: And that he was seen of Cephas, then of the twelve: After that, he was seen of above five hundred brethren at once; of whom the greater part remain unto this present, but some are fallen asleep."

—1 Corinthians 15:1-6

- Notice Paul is going to tell us the Gospel by which we are saved. Paul delivered unto them that which he also believed—the Gospel.

- All the things Paul shared in this passage made it clear that they were according to the Scriptures. They weren't His own thoughts. Remember that all Scripture is given by the inspiration of God (2 Timothy 3:16-17).

Chapter Two

1. Christ

    a) This is a reference to the deity of Jesus, the anointed Messiah.

    b) For one to be born again, they must believe that Jesus is the Son of God. In other words, Jesus is God manifest in the flesh (1 Timothy 3:16). He was not just a good man. He was and is God.

        i) *"Jesus heard that they had cast him out; and when he had found him, he said unto him, Dost thou believe on the Son of God?"* –John 9:35

        ii) *"And we believe and are sure that thou art that Christ, the Son of the living God."* –John 6:69

2. Died and was buried

    "And when Jesus had cried with a loud voice, he said, Father, into thy hands I commend my spirit: and having said thus, he gave up the ghost."

    –Luke 23:46

    a) Some people do not believe that Jesus died. They believe that He fainted or just passed out. That is not what the Scripture teaches (1 Corinthians 15:1-5; Romans 10:9; Mark 15:37; John 19:30).

    b) As a matter of fact, we do not embalm people who have fainted or are in a coma. Jesus' body was *embalmed* because He was dead, and they were trying to preserve it from decaying and decomposition using spices.

        i) *"And there came also Nicodemus, which at the first came to Jesus by night, and brought a mixture of myrrh and aloes, about an hundred pound weight. Then took they the body of Jesus, and wound it in linen clothes with the spices, as the manner of the Jews is to bury."* –John 19:39-40

        ii) *"Now upon the first day of the week, very early in the morning, they came unto the sepulchre, bringing the spices which they had prepared, and certain others with them."* –Luke 24:1

- iii) The mixture of myrrh, aloes, and the spices were for embalming and fragrance purposes.
  - ○ The reason they did not embalm right away was that it was the Sabbath (Mark 16:1).

What do we do with a dead body? We bury it. Jesus was buried because He was dead.

- c) Jesus died bodily. Jesus laid down His life for us (John 10:15-17). He did not resist death, although He could have. He came to die.
- d) He gave up His Spirit and died.
  - i) Giving up the ghost or spirit (Genesis 25:8, 17) is in reference to death. Jesus died.
- e) Jesus was buried in a tomb (sepulcher or grave). People who aren't dead do not live in tombs because they are for burial.
- f) Jesus was also wrapped, which is only done to a dead body.

3. Our sins
   - a) If you do not believe you are a sinner who needs saving, you cannot be born again.
     - i) Jesus died for our sins because we all were sinners.
     - ii) You must acknowledge your need for a Savior to believe and profit from that salvation.
   - b) "For all have sinned, and come short of the glory of God." –Romans 3:23
     - i) No matter how good you might be, you have sinned and have come short of the glory of God–Jesus.
   - c) Note that Jesus died for our sins, not His.

Chapter Two

i) Jesus was sinless (Isaiah 53:9; Hebrews 7:26; John 8:46; 2 Corinthians 5:21; 1 Peter 2:22; and 1 John 3:5)

ii) If Jesus were a sinner, then you could not be born again. You must believe that Jesus was sinless to be born again because if He was a sinner, He couldn't be your Savior.

4. Rose again/Resurrection

"And the angel answered and said unto the women, Fear not ye: for I know that ye seek Jesus, which was crucified. He is not here: for he is risen, as he said. Come, see the place where the Lord lay. And go quickly, and tell his disciples that he is risen from the dead; and, behold, he goeth before you into Galilee; there shall ye see him: lo, I have told you. And they departed quickly from the sepulchre with fear and great joy; and did run to bring his disciples word. And as they went to tell his disciples, behold, Jesus met them, saying, All hail. And they came and held him by the feet, and worshipped him."

–Matthew 28:5-9

a) Jesus died and rose again. He could not have risen again if He had not died in the first place.

i) He rose again bodily and physically–not spiritually, like some people believe.

ii) *"And that he was seen of Cephas, then of the twelve: After that, he was seen of above five hundred brethren at once; of whom the greater part remain unto this present, but some are fallen asleep."* –1 Corinthians 15:5-6

iii) They were able to see Him because He bodily rose. A spirit cannot be seen. If Jesus was a phony, He would have said that He will rise from the dead spiritually, hence leaving no evidence for His resurrection.

No one can be born again unless they believe that Jesus rose again from the dead. This is a crucial aspect of the Gospel.

b) *"That if thou shalt confess with thy mouth the Lord Jesus, and shalt **believe in thine heart that God hath raised him from the dead**, thou shalt be saved."* –Romans 10:9 (emphasis mine)

   i) These verses say that we must believe with the heart. Both head knowledge and acknowledgment are not believing. After we have believed with the heart, then are we to confess. Just confession will not save a person. This has to be a heart commitment and belief.

   ii) We need to profess or confess what we possess.

   iii) If we have truly believed, we will confess as a result of that conviction and love. It is impossible for one to believe on the Lord Jesus and never say they do. True faith will be seen in confession and behavior. The heart is a place of beliefs while the head is a place of thoughts.

   iv) We do not become righteous by performance, but by believing. We can't work our way into righteousness with God.

   v) Romans 10:9-10. Two main things we need to believe to be saved.

   - Who He is and was (Lord Jesus)
     - Lord (Divinity)
     - Jesus (Humanity)

Note: Every cult gets the person of Jesus wrong.

   - What He did
     - Died and rose from the dead–"Believe in thine heart that God hath raised him from the dead"

The Gospel is incomplete without the four parts. Christ, Died for our sins, was buried, and rose again. We must believe all the aspects of the Gospel to truly be born again. We can't believe one and reject another. For instance, if you don't believe that Jesus rose from the dead, you can't be saved even though you believe He died on the cross.

Chapter Three

Can a Christian "Lose" his Salvation or Depart from the Faith?

The Bible expressly warns that some will depart from the faith. Although, some do not believe it is possible to renounce their faith, the Word of God reveals that this is possible, which is a sign of the end times without a doubt. Therefore, we should be careful not to depart from the faith because there remains no more offering for sin. Once one departs from the faith, he or she becomes an apostate. He is a reprobate (one who is worthless, unapproved and rejected–Strong's Concordance) or simply a person rejected by God and beyond hope of salvation.

Every man has free will whether they are born again or not. Believers do not relinquish or lose their free will after they are born again. They can choose to believe in the Lord or they can choose to reject their faith. Our will can be yielded to God, but we still retain it.

For instance, in the New Testament, the following people departed from the faith:

a) Judas (John 6:70-71)

b) Demas (2 Timothy 4:10)

c) Hymenaeus and Alexander (1 Timothy 1:19-20)

GOT QUESTIONS?

An understanding of the answer to this question will also address two common sayings, "Once saved always saved" and another "born again, then born again, again."

I have heard an argument made by some that by no means can a "true believer" renounce their faith or blaspheme the Holy Spirit, but that is not true. This argument cites examples like Romans 11:29, Romans 8:30, Ephesians 1:13-14, Romans 5:1, 1 Peter 1:18-18, and 2 Corinthians 5:17. Although, they have a strong point, it is only argued from one side—God's side. The side of the believer is not addressed, which Hebrews 6:4-6 and Matthew 12:31 clearly address and teach. Their argument eliminates the fact that people willfully believe and can willfully disbelieve or reject their faith.

Although God wants people to stay in a relationship with Him, people can choose to depart or renounce it. It is not a forced relationship with no more choices. The Lord will not cast anyone away from this relationship (John 6:37), but we can walk away from it, renounce or totally reject it. It must be made clear again that it is not just any sin that will cause one to "lose" their salvation, renounce or totally reject it. What it will do is start them on that road to where their heart will be hardened and will reject their faith. We do not lose our salvation because we sinned. If that is true, then none of us would be saved because we have sinned after we got saved.

A true believer cannot lose his salvation like you lose a wallet. You can't wake up one day and wonder where your salvation is or what happened to it. The word "lose" is better described by the words "fall away", "depart from", "renounce" and/or "blasphemy of the Holy Spirit."

You can either totally renounce your salvation or blaspheme the Holy Spirit, but suicide, murder, and adultery cannot void your salvation. For you to *lose* your salvation, you would have to totally renounce it.

You cannot sin away your salvation because all sin is paid for: past, present and future sins (Hebrews 10:12, 14). If sin can cause you to lose your salvation, then which sin is it? Why that specific sin and not another? We do not lose, fall away from, reject, renounce or depart from our salvation every time we sin.

Chapter Three

Unpardonable sin

Besides the total rejecting or renouncing of one's salvation, the other way one can "lose", depart from, and totally reject the faith and salvation is by blaspheming the Holy Spirit.

> "Wherefore I say unto you, All manner of sin and blasphemy shall be forgiven unto men: but the blasphemy against the Holy Ghost shall not be forgiven unto men."
>
> –Matthew 12:31

a) The word "blaspheme" means attributing the work of the Holy Spirit to the devil, to revile. It is vilification, especially against God. (Strong's Concordance).

To blaspheme is defined by Thayer's definitions as slander, detraction, speech injurious, to another's good name; impious and reproachful speech injurious to divine majesty.

b) In this situation of blaspheming as well as the renouncing and total rejection of faith, the same indicators of Hebrews 6:4-6 also apply. Only a person who is mature in the Lord is capable of rejecting their salvation. Blasphemy done ignorantly in unbelief is excused and is not counted against that person. This blasphemy against the Holy Spirit must be done willfully with knowledge of what is being done. In 1 Timothy 1:13, Paul said that he reviled (blasphemed) and he spoke against the Holy Spirit ignorantly in unbelief but received mercy. Matthew 12:31 further attests to the deity of the Holy Spirit, seeing that this sin committed against Him shall not be forgiven.

> "For if we sin wilfully after that we have received the knowledge of the truth, remaineth no more sacrifice for sins, But a certain fearful looking for of judgment and fiery indignation, which shall devour the adversaries."
>
> –Hebrews 10:26-27

When we get born again, we do it by exercising our free will. We do not lose our free will because we are now saved. We still retain it. In the same way, believers can exercise their free will to reject their salvation or to blaspheme the Holy Spirit. Although, the Lord does not desire this, and the results are extremely severe and irreversible, a Christian believer can still do it. True, every sin a person commits is willful; however, these verses are specifically talking about the willful sin of renouncing the Lord and/or blaspheming against the Holy Spirit, not sin in general.

> *"If it were true that after we are born again we lose our salvation when we sin and we are "backslid" and are in a damned state until we repent and get back into salvation, then the best thing to do would be to kill all new converts as soon as they were saved. That would be the only way they could ever retain their salvation. That is a foolish religious doctrine."*
>
> —Andrew Wommack, Living Commentary

1. *"As ye have therefore received Christ Jesus the Lord, so walk ye in him:"* – Colossians 2:6

   The question I have for you is, how did you receive the Lord Jesus Christ? It was through faith. You put your trust and faith in the Lord. You did not perform or do all these good deeds to receive the Lord. It was purely faith in the Lord. In the same way you received, it is the same way you are supposed to walk, and it is the same way you can choose to depart from the faith.

2. *"For it is impossible for those who were once enlightened, and have tasted of the heavenly gift, and were made partakers of the Holy Ghost, And have tasted the good word of God, and the powers of the world to come, If they shall fall away, to renew them again unto repentance; seeing they crucify to themselves the Son of God afresh, and put him to an open shame."* –Hebrews 6:4-5

    A. These verses make it clear that it is impossible for a person who meets the above requirements to be renewed or restored back unto faith in the Lord Jesus Christ. If we renounce our faith, we can't be renewed again into faith in Jesus as our Lord. In other words, we can't be saved again.

Chapter Three

B. It is impossible to be born again, again. These verses prove that a Christian can depart from or renounce their salvation. These passages are talking about the rejection of salvation or blasphemy. It is possible that one can reject their salvation. Once that person does, he cannot be restored back into their relationship with God. He becomes a reprobate and is given over to a reprobate mind (Romans 1:28).

C. When we were born again, we weren't forced, nor are we forced to stay born again. We chose to enter into and accept this relationship with God by simply believing, and we exit by just disbelieving or rejecting our salvation.

   a) We have an eternal redemption and we have been sanctified and perfected once and for all.

      i) *"And being made perfect, he became the author of eternal salvation unto all them that obey him;"* –Hebrews 5:9

      ii) *"Neither by the blood of goats and calves, but by his own blood he entered in once into the holy place,* **having obtained eternal redemption** *for us."* –Hebrews 9:12 (emphasis mine)

      iii) *"And for this cause he is the mediator of the new testament, that by means of death, for the redemption of the transgressions that were under the first testament, they which are called might receive the promise of eternal inheritance."* –Hebrews 9:15

      iv) *"So Christ was once offered to bear the sins of many; and unto them that look for him shall he appear the second time without sin unto salvation."* –Hebrews 9:28

      v) *"By the which will we are sanctified through the offering of the body of Jesus Christ* **once for all**.*"* –Hebrews 10:10 (emphasis mine)

      vi) *"But this man, after he had* **offered one sacrifice for sins for ever**, *sat down on the right hand of God;"* –Hebrews 10:12 (emphasis mine)

      vii) *"For by one offering he hath* **perfected for ever** *them that are* **sanctified**.*"* –Hebrews 10:14 (emphasis mine)

D. Sin is not the reason we lose our salvation. We don't just sin it away. We disbelieve it away or reject and renounce it. We did not get saved by our actions and we do not lose salvation by our actions.

E. There are five qualifications that these verses give that must be met before a Christian can become reprobate having renounced his salvation, but close attention to these five guidelines reveals that very few Christian believers could meet these qualifications because these verses do not describe an immature believer, but one who is mature.

The five requirements are:

   a) "Once enlightened" refers to those who have once had a revelation of Jesus to them through the Holy Spirit–John 6:44-45.

   b) "Tasted of the heavenly gift"–this is a reference to the salvation gift, not religion or religious practices.

      i) *"For by grace are ye saved through faith; and that not of yourselves: it is the gift of God:"* –Ephesians 2:8.

   c) "Were made partakers of the Holy Ghost" refers to receiving the gift of the Holy Spirit.

   d) "Have tasted the good word of God" refers to revelation knowledge of God's Word.

   e) The powers of the world to come–supernatural power and the gifts of the Holy Spirit.

F. This renouncing of the faith cannot be done by any believer, such as a baby Christian. These qualifications and/or requirements can only be met by a mature believer.

   a) An immature Christian will not be held for this sin in the same way a child is not held for certain sins if they aren't old enough. Once they are old enough, they will be held responsible for their

Chapter Three

behavior–from that point going forward having reached the age of accountability.

Hebrews 6:6 explains that once a person who is mature in the Lord willfully rejects the Lord (falls away), knowing what he is doing, he can't be saved again (born again, again). Our sins were paid for once (Hebrews 10:12, 14). If we reject it, there is no more sacrifice for our sins. There is no recovery from renouncing our faith in Jesus. Our fate is sealed.

All these requirements or indicators are pointing to a mature Christian, not an immature Christian like Paul was when he blasphemed the Holy Spirit ignorantly and in unbelief (1 Timothy 1:13). This removes the fear that could be operating in some who might think that they lost their salvation, blasphemed the Holy Spirit and/or renounced their faith.

If you still have a heart and love for the Lord, you are not a reprobate. You have not departed nor renounced your faith. If you still have a longing to pursue and seek after the Lord, you have not "lost" your salvation. If it so happens that you have renounced the Lord, blasphemed against the Holy Spirit or departed from the faith, you will have zero desire for the Lord and the things of the Lord. You will have pleasure in doing filthy, ungodly things. You will increase in committing unrighteousness. You will be completely immoral with no remorse and zero desire to change. You will be completely given over to your reprobate mind.

"And changed the glory of the uncorruptible God into an image made like to corruptible man, and to birds, and fourfooted beasts, and creeping things. Wherefore God also gave them up to uncleanness through the lusts of their own hearts, to dishonour their own bodies between themselves: Who changed the truth of God into a lie, and worshipped and served the creature more than the Creator, who is blessed forever. Amen. For this cause God gave them up unto vile affections: for even their women did change the natural use into that which is against nature: And likewise also the men, leaving the natural use of the woman, burned in their lust one toward another; men with men working that which is unseemly, and receiving in themselves that recompence of their error which was meet. And even as they did not like to retain God in their knowledge, God gave them over to a reprobate mind, to do those things which are not convenient; Being

filled with all unrighteousness, fornication, wickedness, covetousness, maliciousness; full of envy, murder, debate, deceit, malignity; whisperers, Backbiters, haters of God, despiteful, proud, boasters, inventors of evil things, disobedient to parents, Without understanding, covenant breakers, without natural affection, implacable, unmerciful: Who knowing the judgment of God, that they which commit such things are worthy of death, not only do the same, but have pleasure in them that do them."

–Romans 1:23-32

"Reprobate" refers to a sinner who has lost all conviction of God, unrepentant, beyond rescue, and has been given over to do those things that are unspeakable. One who is rejected, unapproved and cast away.

We also see from these verses that once someone departs from the faith either through renouncing or blasphemy against the Holy Spirit, he is unrepentant, has pleasure in doing evil, wickedness, and sin although he knows the judgment of God to come. He doesn't care and does not like to retain God in his knowledge for which God gives him or her over to a reprobate mind, to do those things which are not convenient and righteous.

3. *"If we confess our sins, he is faithful and just to forgive us our sins, and to cleanse us from all unrighteousness."* –1 John 1:9.

   A. Although it is important to confess our sins, some have erroneously taught that if we do not confess our sins and get born again, *again*, we wouldn't make it to heaven, but to hell. Are we to confess our sins or confess Jesus? Which is the priority?

   B. This teaching makes our salvation dependent on confessing all our sins to make it to heaven which no one can practically and accurately do. In return, this has destroyed people's faith because no one has ever fully and completely confessed each and every sin in their lives.

   C. We are to confess Jesus as our Lord (Romans 10:9-10. Additionally, why then did Jesus die on the cross if all it took was confessing our sins to go to heaven?

Chapter Three

    D. It takes believing, receiving, and confessing Jesus, not confessing our sin, to enter into a relationship with the Lord.

4. *"Now the Spirit speaketh expressly, that in the latter times some shall depart from the faith, giving heed to seducing spirits, and doctrines of devils;"* –1 Timothy 4:1

    A. Some shall depart from the faith

        a) How can someone depart from the faith he has never had? You cannot depart from something you aren't a part of, and you can't even do so if you had no free will to do so.

        b) Depart means to "remove, desist, desert."

            i) The word "depart" used here signifies someone walking away from something, which in this case is salvation.

            ii) This verse clearly indicates that one can depart from the faith, but you cannot depart from something that you have never had. So, this Scripture among many others disproves the doctrine of "once saved, always saved."

            iii) This is a result of giving heed to seducing spirits and doctrines of the devils. See 1 Tim 4:1.

5. *"Let us hold fast the profession of our faith without wavering; (for he is faithful that promised)."* –Hebrews 10:23

    A. Hold fast the profession of our faith without wavering.

        a) Hold fast means "to hold down."

        b) The Greek word for "profession" is *homologia*, which means acknowledgment.

            i) Is it possible that someone can waver? If it was impossible, this passage would not have told us to hold on our faith without wavering.

            ii) Why hold fast onto something you can't lose or depart from?

Again, this passage instructs us to hold fast but it would not have said so if there was no need for doing so.

6. *"Who concerning the truth have erred, saying that the resurrection is past already; and overthrow the faith of some." –2 Timothy 2:18.*

    A. "Who concerning the truth have erred."

        a) Based on this passage, it is possible to err concerning the truth or the faith. We must continually renew our minds and stay away from doctrines of devils.

    B. Saying that the resurrection is past already."

        a) The resurrection is not over and done with. There remains a resurrection of the saints at the second coming of the Lord (1 Thessalonians 4:13-18).

        b) If the resurrection has already taken place, then this also is suggesting that the return of the Lord has already taken place.

        c) This teaching or belief of some also takes away the comfort that comes from the Scriptures concerning the resurrection.

    C. "Overthrow the faith of some"

        a) Overthrow means "to overturn."

            i) Bad or demonic doctrines can cause the faith of many to be overturned.

            ii) How can the faith of some be overthrown if once saved is always saved? There are things that believers can do that will lead them to a place of departing, renouncing their faith. They can become reprobates according to Romans 1:23-28 and Hebrews 3:12-13.

            iii) The just shall live by faith and we must endure to the end, holding onto our faith in the Lord Jesus Christ.

Chapter Three

7. *"Fight the good fight of faith, lay hold on eternal life, whereunto thou art also called, and hast professed a good profession before many witnesses."* –1 Timothy 6:12

    A. Why should we hold on to eternal life if we can't depart from it? There would be no need for holding on, right? Right.

    These verses below are parallel to Hebrews 6:4-6:

    a) *"For if we sin wilfully after that we have received the knowledge of the truth, there remaineth no more sacrifice for sins, But a certain fearful looking for of judgment and fiery indignation, which shall devour the adversaries. He that despised Moses' law died without mercy under two or three witnesses: Of how much sorer punishment, suppose ye, shall he be thought worthy, who hath trodden under foot the Son of God, and hath counted the blood of the covenant, wherewith he was sanctified, an unholy thing, and hath done despite unto the Spirit of grace?"* –Hebrews 10:26-29

    b) *"Wherefore I say unto you, All manner of sin and blasphemy shall be forgiven unto men: but the blasphemy against the Holy Ghost shall not be forgiven unto men. And whosoever speaketh a word against the Son of man, it shall be forgiven him: but whosoever speaketh against the Holy Ghost, it shall not be forgiven him, neither in this world, neither in the world to come."* –Matthew 12:31-32

There is a caution I want to leave with you. If you choose to live a sinful, ungodly, and unrepentant lifestyle, you will harden your heart to the Lord (Hebrews 3:13). Living in this continual state and lifestyle will get a believer to a place and position so far away and disconnected from the Lord that he will be presented with an opportunity from Satan to renounce and totally reject their faith or even blasphemy of the Holy Spirit. Neither of these sins (total rejection and renouncing of the faith and blasphemy against the Holy Spirit) just happen overnight. It is a continual state of mind and lifestyle that eventually leads to someone totally rejecting their faith.

Chapter Four

Why live a godly life? Are there any benefits of living a godly life?

The vertical effects of sin between God and man have been dealt with. The problem still lies between men–horizontally. Although, living in sin is terrible and very dangerous, it doesn't stop God from loving us. God loves us unconditionally. Sin is no longer a barrier between you and God. It has been paid for in FULL. It's no longer a barrier. Jesus paid it all and there is none left to pay for.

If God cannot love someone who sins, He has no one to love because we all come short (Romans 3:23). If God cannot hear a prayer of someone with some sort of sin in their life, then God cannot hear any prayer because none of us measure up in our performance. That said, it is not an excuse to live that way. If a person doesn't live a godly life, it is inaccurate to say that they love God while they live like the devil.

Our actions are important, but they do not earn us right standing with God. They do not produce salvation nor earn us extra favor and points with God. Our actions are not what please God, but faith (Hebrews 11:6). It is our faith in Jesus that produces righteousness and right standing with God, not our actions. The Lord loves us unconditionally and His blessings and love for us are not proportional to our performance. Thank You, Jesus! Although we receive all God has for us by grace and we are pure and sinless in our born-again Spirit (Ephesians 4:24; 1 John 3:6; 3:9; and Ephesians 1:13), we also have a physical body and a soul that we use to relate to people in this world. The way God sees us in the Spirit is not the way the world does. We do not relate to people spirit to spirit, nor do they see our born-again spirits.

Horizontally, here in this life and the world we live in, our actions are extremely important for relationships and other good things. If we ignore good actions here on earth, we lose our influence and ability to go further. No one wants to deal with someone bad. "Sin (or living an ungodly life) will cost you more than you want to pay, take you further than you want to go, and keep you longer than you want to stay." –*Pastor Lawson Perdue*

God loves us, but does not love or approve of everything we do. Study the Word. Paul continually instructed believers against living ungodly. It is detrimental to us. God loves us and wants us to experience the victory He has for us, but that does not come through living contrary to His Word.

God blesses and delights in us, but He does not bless nor delight in everything we do. God does not have pleasure in things that are against His will. God is for us (Romans 8:31), but is not for everything we do. God died for all our sins but does not delight in them. Let everyone that nameth the name of Christ depart from iniquity. (2 Timothy 2:19)

We are candidates of Heaven through faith in Jesus Christ, but in this life, we will experience greater measures of hell if we do not live godly.

In this chapter, I want to encourage you to pursue and live a godly life. It is just the right thing to do and if you are born again, it is your nature to live godly. I'm not advocating behavior modification, but a relationship with Jesus that has the fruit of good behavior, actions, and lifestyle. Behavior modification is not equivalent to Christianity. If you aren't born again, you must be (John 3:3). A change in behavior doesn't produce salvation. Even if a person were able to live a godly life outwardly, it doesn't mean they are born again.

"I beseech you, therefore, brethren, by the mercies of God [grace of God], that ye present your bodies a living sacrifice, holy, acceptable unto God, which is your reasonable service."

–Romans 12:1

Chapter Four

Paul never used scare tactics or the wrath of God to get people to live godly. He motivated them by the grace and mercies of God. Notice that he beseeched them, not commanded them nor forced them. Loving God and knowing His love for you, will cause you to live godlier accidentally than you ever have on purpose. The best Bible that unbelievers could ever read is your lifestyle. Our actions speak louder than words. They speak so loudly that many people can't hear what we are saying.

"Wherefore, my beloved, as ye have always obeyed, not as in my presence only, but now much more in my absence, work out your own salvation with fear and trembling."
–Philippians 2:12

This verse tells us to work out our salvation, not to work for it. When we work out our salvation, we are exercising and/or manifesting that which is already a reality on the inside of us working it to the outside.

According to 2 Timothy 3:12 and 1 Peter 4:12-16, he who lives a godly life or a different life from the world, will be persecuted for their faith. If you never bump into the devil, it's probably because you are headed in the same direction. As long as you are swimming upstream, you will find resistance.

Below I list some of the key reasons we want to live a godly life or why our good actions matter.

a) Sensitivity to God

"But exhort one another daily, while it is called Today; lest any of you be hardened through the deceitfulness of sin."
–Hebrews 3:13

People who are sensitive to God are not living a life of ungodliness. Living an ungodly life deadens your sensitivity toward God–it hardens your heart toward God. Every time someone manifests a pattern of good works, it increases their sensitivity toward God because they are submitted and in agreement with the Lord through their actions. Sin or ungodly lifestyle deceives our hearts. It makes our hearts unfeeling, cold, and unyielding to the Lord.

b) Evidence of a changed life and salvation

This is one of the most important reasons for living a godly life or having good deeds.

"For we are his workmanship, created in Christ Jesus unto good works, which God hath before ordained that we should walk in them."

–Ephesians 2:10.

"Ye shall know them by their fruits. Do men gather grapes of thorns, or figs of thistles?"

–Matthew 7:16, 20

If I have a pineapple sign on me, yet I am producing apples, what are you going to believe? My sign or what I'm producing? We were created unto good works, not unto ungodliness. We can't just profess to know the Lord unless our actions say the same thing. Our actions are the fruit and proof of our relationship with the Lord, not the root. As important as our actions are, they do not produce salvation. Only faith in what Christ Jesus did for us can produce true salvation. But true salvation must make a difference in a person's life by changing and influencing their behavior.

The evidence of our changed life is not just the words we say, but the life we conduct or what the Bible calls our conversation. Relationship with Christ Jesus must be backed by a change in our lifestyle or else we are liars. Many people can say that they are born-again believers or Christians, but the way they live reflects something else. We as children of God ought to live like Jesus, not like the devil.

For many Christians, they say one thing and their actions say another. They are so loud with their words that we can't hear them. If most

Chapter Four

Christians were arrested for being Christians, there wouldn't be enough evidence to convict them. That's an indication that we aren't living like Christians because there isn't any proof of those Christian claims.

"In all things shewing thyself a pattern of good works: *in doctrine shewing uncorruptness, gravity, sincerity, sound speech, that cannot be condemned; that he that is of the contrary part may be ashamed, having no evil thing to say of you."*

–Titus 2:7-8

This verse is also admonishing us to have a pattern of good works noticeable in all things (such as sincerity, sound speech, and so forth) to the point that we cannot be condemned and without reproach or anything negative laid against us. People are watching you if you claim you are a born-again Christian. They expect you to live, behave a certain way. Your lifestyle will either draw people to the Lord or from the Lord (1Peter 2:12). To some people, you are the only Bible they will ever read. You are the written epistle that others do read.

Our actions are so important in this life (1Peter 2:15). They either open doors for us or shut them. We can't just live the way we want or like anyone else, because we are Christians (Acts 11:26) and there is a standard set by our Lord through His Word, a standard required of all of us, not just pastors, preachers, and teachers. In an effort to become great preachers, we should not become lousy Christians. There are things we do not want to do and places we do not want to go because of who we are.

c) Yield to God or Satan

   i) *"Know ye not, that to whom ye yield yourselves servants to obey, his servants ye are to whom ye obey; whether of sin unto death, or of obedience unto righteousness?"*– Romans 6:16

   - Sin is like sewage that attracts flies.

- ii) *"The thief cometh not, but for to steal, and to kill, and to destroy: I am come that they might have life, and that they might have it more abundantly."* – John 10:10

    - Living an ungodly lifestyle opens up a door to the devil to come into our lives and steal, kill, and destroy.

d) Exemplary life

- i) *"Let no man despise thy youth; but be thou an example of the believers, in word, in conversation, in charity, in spirit, in faith, in purity."* – 1 Timothy 4:12

    - We are admonished to be an example to the believers in our behavior (conversation). If we are going to be leaders, we ought to have godly influence. When we live a life that doesn't reflect Jesus Christ, our influence goes out of the window and our respect goes out through the door.

- ii) *"Brethren, be followers together of me, and mark them which walk so as ye have us for an ensample."* – Philippians 3:17

- iii) *"Be ye followers of me, even as I also am of Christ."* – 1 Corinthians 11:1

    - Just like the Christians in Antioch (Acts 11:26), there is a way a Christian believer ought to live. People have certain expectations from Christians. What we watch, what we listen to, how we dress, and how we talk ought to be exemplary. There ought to be a difference between a Christian believer and a nonbeliever.

e) Temple of the Holy Spirit

- i) *"What? know ye not that he which is joined to an harlot is one body? for two, saith he, shall be one flesh. But he that is joined unto the Lord is one spirit. Flee fornication. Every sin that a man doeth is without the body; but he that committeth fornication sinneth against his own body.*

Chapter Four

What? know ye not that your body is the temple of the Holy Ghost which is in you, which ye have of God, and ye are not your own? For ye are bought with a price: therefore, glorify God in your body, and in your spirit, which are God's."– 1 Corinthians 6:16-20

- ii) *"And what agreement hath the temple of God with idols? for ye are the temple of the living God; as God hath said, I will dwell in them, and walk in them; and I will be their God, and they shall be my people."* –2 Corinthians 6:16

    - Because God dwells in us, we are the temple of the Holy Spirit. If only we treated our bodies as the temple of the Holy Spirit and as a member of Christ's body, we would think twice about doing what we ought not to do. Our body is a member of Christ's body. If this is true, which it is, then you are dragging the Lord into all the sin and immorality that you get involved in.

f) Missed opportunities such as promotion, open doors, and growth

- i) *"A bishop then must be blameless, the husband of one wife, vigilant, sober, **of good behaviour**, given to hospitality, apt to teach;* [7] *Moreover he must have a **good report of them which are without**; lest he fall into reproach and the snare of the devil."* (Emphasis mine). –1 Timothy 3:2, 7

    - Although living a godly life, having good deeds doesn't make you better than your neighbor, it puts you in a better position than them. No one wants to hire or promote a talebearer, scorner, pervert, a thief, or a slob. Many believers wonder why every time promotion comes around; they don't get it. They wonder why no one wants to promote them but the reason is apparent.

g) Sending the devil to flight (Resisting the devil)

- i) *Submit yourselves therefore to God. Resist the devil, and he will flee from you.* –James 4:7

- You can't resist what you are submitted to. A lack of good behavior is a submission to Satan. This renders you ineffective to rid yourself of the enemy.

h) Causes poverty

Sin is expensive! Living ungodly lifestyles is too costly. Sinful acts will run you broke. Divorce, jail, and so forth could be the result of such behaviors.

   i) *"He that loveth pleasure shall be a poor man: he that loveth wine and oil shall not be rich."* – Proverbs 21:17

   ii) *"For the drunkard and the glutton shall come to poverty: and drowsiness shall clothe a man with rags."* – Proverbs 23:21

   iii) *"Whoso loveth wisdom rejoiceth his father: but he that keepeth company with harlots spendeth his substance."* – Proverbs 29:3

i) Shortens life

   i) *"What man is he that desireth life, and loveth many days, that he may see good? Keep thy tongue from evil, and thy lips from speaking guile. Depart from evil, and do good; seek peace, and pursue it."* – Psalm 34:12-14, 21

   ii) *"A sound heart is the life of the flesh: but envy the rottenness of the bones."* – Proverbs 14:30

   iii) *"Honour thy father and thy mother: that thy days may be long upon the land which the Lord thy God giveth thee."* – Exodus 20:12

   iv) *"Depart from evil, and do good; and dwell for evermore."* – Psalm 37:27

   v) *"The fear of the Lord is a fountain of life, to depart from the snares of death."* – Proverbs 14:27

j) The revelation of forgiveness

Chapter Four

- i) *"Wherefore I say unto thee, Her sins, which are many, are forgiven; for she loved much: but to whom **little** is forgiven, the same **loveth little**."* (emphasis mine).– Luke 7:47

    - One of the reasons people continue to struggle with sin in their lives and its stronghold is because of the lack of the revelation of forgiveness.
    - This verse points out that he who is forgiven much loves much and he who is forgiven little, the same loveth little.
    - The degree to which we renew our minds to the enormous forgiveness we have received from Jesus; we will walk in the abundance of life and it will break the power of sin in our lives.

k) A changed nature and a new identity in Christ.

Once a person becomes born-again, he receives a new identity. He has a new ID. He must live his new life with this new ID as his point of reference and the very thing to show to anyone who questions who they are. This new ID is *"who they are in Christ."* We are supposed to see ourselves no more by the old ID but only with the new ID. We want to live a godly life because of who we are. We have a changed nature.

- i) *"God forbid. How shall we, that are dead to sin, live any longer therein?"*-Romans 6:2

- ii) *"For he that is dead is freed from sin."*-Romans 6:7

- iii) *"For we are his workmanship, created in Christ Jesus unto good works, which God hath before ordained that we should walk in them."*-Ephesians 2:10

- iv) Children of Light

    "For ye were sometimes darkness, but now are ye light in the Lord: walk as children of light"

    –Ephesians 5:8

- Knowing who we are in Christ is one of the major keys to breaking the stronghold of sin and stopping it from reigning in our lives. A lack thereof is one of the reasons many still struggle. If you are a believer, you need to learn to see yourself in Christ.

- The way we see ourselves is what we will be and how we will act. If a person can change their inner image of themselves, they can change how they act.

v) *"Beloved, now are we the sons of God, and it doth not yet appear what we shall be: but we know that, when he shall appear, we shall be like him; for we shall see him as he is."*–1 John 3:2

- One of the reasons that we shall be like Him when we see Him is because we shall see Him and shall be changed into who we see.

vi) *"But we all, with uncovered face beholding as in a glass the glory of the Lord, are changed into the same image, from glory to glory, even as by the Spirit of the Lord."*–2 Corinthians 3:18

- This verse is clearly stating we become what we behold. We are changed into that same image. Until a Christian sees himself right, he may never ever overcome sin.

vii) *"Know ye not that the unrighteous shall not inherit the kingdom of God? Be not deceived: neither fornicators, nor idolaters, nor adulterers, nor effeminate, nor abusers of themselves with mankind, Nor thieves, nor covetous, nor drunkards, nor revilers, nor extortioners, shall inherit the kingdom of God. And such were some of you: but ye are washed, but ye are sanctified, but ye are justified in the name of the Lord Jesus, and by the Spirit of our God."*–1 Corinthians 6:9-11

- Notice how Paul says, *"And such were some of you: but ye are washed, but ye are sanctified, but ye are justified in the name of the Lord Jesus, and by the Spirit of our God."* Why is he doing this? He was appealing to their new nature and to who these believers were in the Spirit to motivate them and encourage them not to sin like the unbelievers (fornicators, idolaters, adulterers, effeminate, abusers of themselves with mankind, thieves, covetous, drunkards, revilers, extortioners.

Every time Paul dealt with sin in the life of the believer (Galatians 3), he always pointed to who they were in Christ. There are certain things we will never do and certain places we will never go because it is not who we are. There are things I just can't do because of who I am.

The way you are acting is not who you are. That is not you. If you knew, understood, and had the revelation that you were the righteousness of God, then how would you go commit sin? It would be almost impossible. I don't suck my thumb. Why not? Because I'm not an infant. Only infants suck their thumbs.

These verses detail our new identity

i) One spirit with the Lord –1 Corinthians 6:17; Romans 8:9, 8:11

ii) Sealed such that no impurities can penetrate –Ephesians 1:13; 2 Corinthians 1:22

iii) New creation –2 Corinthians 5:17

iv) New Man, New Spirit, righteous and created in true Holiness – Ephesians 4:24

v) As He is, so are we in this world –1 John 4:17

vi) He cannot sin –1 John 3:6; 3:9

vii) Fruit of the Spirit –Gal 5:22-23

viii) Wisdom, righteous, sanctified and redeemed –1 Corinthians 1:30

ix) Eternally redeemed –Hebrews 9:12

x) Has the fullness of God –John 1:16. It is full of the presence of God

xi) Anointed –2 Corinthians 1:21; 1 John 2:27 –Anointing abides in us.

xii) Complete in Him –Col 2:10 –there is no inadequacy in it.

xiii) We have been given all it takes to live a victorious Christian life in this life. 2 Peter 1:3

xiv) Always willing –Matthew 26:41

xv) Perfected forever–Hebrews 10:14, Hebrews 12:23–Spirits of just men made perfect.

xvi) Partaker of the divine nature –2Peter 1:4

xvii) Knows all things–1 Corinthians 2:16.

Many of the problems in our lives can be associated with an ungodly lifestyle. Sin is one of the main causes of all our problems.

The course of Action: Change your mind (repent) and then start renewing it (Romans 12:1-2).

Reminder: God's love for us is not based on how holy we live, but on faith in Jesus as our Lord and Savior.

Chapter Five

What about Tithes and Offerings?

A tithe simply means a tenth. Some people argue for, while others against, the tithe, but I hope this chapter can give you some insights.

Many people think, "I'm struggling already, and if I give 10%, I will be with less not more." Wrong! If you are left with 90%, 90% with God's blessing is more and better than 100% of your money without God's blessing. Furthermore, if 90% is not enough, 100% will not be. Putting God first releases a blessing upon the rest of the 90% and you can do more with that than you would have done with 100%. Putting God first always works.

You do not have to give just 10% to the letter. You can do more as you please. I heard a story of a man of God who gives away almost 80% and lives off just 20%. We should aspire to give more than just tithes because we are so much more blessed than the folks in the Old Testament. While the law of the tithe is no longer in effect, the spiritual principle of promise remains (Luke 6:38, Rom. 11:16).

We are to give tithes, not pay tithes. A tithe is not a debt we owe under the New Covenant, and we should not give with a debt mentality. Abraham gave tithes; he did not pay tithes (Hebrews 7:4). We don't give the tithe out of obligation in the New Testament, but out of love and a revelation of the grace and goodness of God.

A tithe is not a tax. I have heard some people say, that the tithe is a tax from God. This is not biblical rather a perception that people have. A tax may not be willful while the tithe is. Once we give tithes with a wrong motive, it voids our gift. It profits us nothing (1 Corinthians 13:1-3).

I also want to submit to you that not everyone can start by giving 10%. I believe some people need to grow to the place of 10% and beyond. It's better to start where your faith is and build up to 10% and more as you purpose in your heart. It is better for some to start by giving 2% or 5% in faith, love, and with a right heart attitude and motive than give 10% out of a wrong motive, obligation, and compulsion because it will profit them nothing.

Not cursed anymore

"Christ hath redeemed us from the curse of the law, being made a curse for us: for it is written, Cursed is everyone that hangeth on a tree: That the blessing of Abraham might come on the Gentiles through Jesus Christ; that we might receive the promise of the Spirit through faith."

–Galatians 3:13-14

Giving under the New Covenant is different from the Old Covenant. This is a reality we all have to accept. Grace will always give and do more than the law demands. As we support the work of God, such as churches, ministers, and ministries, we release God's provision and promises in our lives. Whenever we do what God has ordained us to do, it releases the promise (Philippians 4:19). We must also abound in this grace of giving, not just in everything else such as faith, utterance, knowledge, love, diligence, etc (2 Corinthians 8:7)

Before the law, the original tithe of the promise had no curse attached to it if one failed. It was all one's free will. Tithing under the New Testament is not under the curse. If you do not give, you will not be cursed. Jesus has redeemed us from the curse of the law (Galatians 3:13). I believe tithing should still be going on under the new covenant, but with a different motive. What needs to change is not your act of giving, but your heart motive and attitude. Being redeemed from the curse of the law doesn't mean you go out and live ungodly. What is right doesn't change, but it's the motive and attitude that needs to change.

The tithe was a spiritual principle before the law was given. It was then given as a law during the law dispensation, and a spiritual principle under the New Covenant of grace.

i) Genesis 14:20, And blessed be the most high God, which hath delivered thine enemies into thy hand. And he gave him tithes of all.

ii) Genesis 28:22, And this stone, which I have set for a pillar, shall be God's house: and of all that thou shalt give me I will surely give the tenth unto thee.

iii) Paul uses the pattern of the law to establish a New Testament principle.

> 1 Corinthians 9:6 *Or I only and Barnabas, have not we power to forbear working? 7 Who goeth a warfare any time at his own charges? who planteth a vineyard, and eateth not of the fruit thereof? or who feedeth a flock, and eateth not of the milk of the flock? 8 Say I these things as a man? or saith not the law the same also? 9 For it is written in the law of Moses, Thou shalt not muzzle the mouth of the ox that treadeth out the corn. Doth God take care for oxen? 10 Or saith he it altogether for our sakes? For our sakes, no doubt, this is written: that he that ploweth should plow in hope; and that he that thresheth in hope should be partaker of his hope. 11 If we have sown unto you spiritual things, is it a great thing if we shall reap your carnal things? 12 If others be partakers of this power over you, are not we rather? Nevertheless we have not used this power; but suffer all things, lest we should hinder the gospel of Christ. 13 Do ye not know that they which minister about holy things live of the things of the temple? and they which wait at the altar are partakers with the altar? 14 Even so hath the Lord ordained that they which preach the gospel should live of the gospel.*

Paul mentions that:

- o   It is written in the Law
- o   It is for our sakes
- o   They which minister 'live of the temple.'
- o   'Even so'……. 'in the same way'…. they which preach the Gospel should live of the Gospel.

Based on 1 Corinthians 9:6-14, here is a question to those that say the tithe has been abolished under the New Covenant. How can the tithe be abolished in the New Testament when Paul is using the same pattern under that law to set into motion a New Testament principle? What was it that they which ministered in the temple lived off of? It was the tithes. The tithes mentioned in Malachi 3:10 were given to the ones ministering as their compensation or support, in the same way, they that minister (preach the Gospel) under the New Testament live off the giving of the tithes.

Preachers of the Gospel should live of the Gospel

"Do ye not know that they which minister about holy things live of the things of the temple? and they which wait at the altar are partakers with the altar? Even so hath the Lord ordained that they which preach the Gospel should live of the Gospel."

–1 Corinthians 9:13-14

God has ordained that the preachers of the Gospel, should live off the Gospel, but how can they if we do not tithe systematically and continuously? This does not say preachers should live off the Gospel, but those who preach the Gospel (the too good to be true, the grace of God), not the law and damnation. Not all preachers are preaching the Gospel. Recently the Lord spoke to me to start giving to my own ministry. I believe this is in line with this passage. Pastors and other ministers all give to their ministries. This will be a huge revelation to many ministers.

Chapter Five

Minister

"Now he that ministereth seed to the sower both minister bread for your food, and multiply your seed sown, and increase the fruits of your righteousness."

—2 Corinthians 9:10

God supplies us with seed to sow and food to eat. He gives us seed to plant and makes the seed grow or increase. Notice that God only multiplies the seed that you sow or release into the Kingdom. If we want our seed to multiply, we must release it into the Kingdom. It does not multiply in your wallet or pocket, rather in the ground. God is in the multiplication business, not the addition business and when it comes to sown seed, what you give, you get to keep. If you are a sower, God will get seed to you.

"Will a man rob God? Yet ye have robbed me. But ye say, wherein have we robbed thee? In tithes and offerings. 9 Ye are cursed with a curse: for ye have robbed me, even this whole nation. 10 Bring ye all the tithes into the storehouse, that there may be meat in mine house, and prove me now herewith, saith the LORD of hosts, if I will not open you the windows of heaven, and pour you out a blessing, that there shall not be room enough to receive it.

—Malachi 3:8-10

According to Malachi 3:8, those who are opposed to the giving of the tithe in the New Testament should equally be opposed to the offering because they are both commanded in the same passage of Scripture.

If it is wrong to tithe, it is equally wrong to give an offering. It is hypocritical to ask for offerings and yet at the same time, condemn tithing as being a part of the law. Additionally, if there is a curse on not tithing, there is equally a curse on not giving offerings.

These verses do not just speak of not tithing as robbing God, but reveal that if we do not give offerings, we are robing God as well. We can't just choose to speak of tithes alone.

Store house

"Will a man rob God? Yet ye have robbed me. But ye say, wherein have we robbed thee? In tithes and offerings. 9 Ye are cursed with a curse: for ye have robbed me, even this whole nation. 10 Bring ye all the tithes into the storehouse, that there may be meat in mine house, and prove me now herewith, saith the LORD of hosts, if I will not open you the windows of heaven, and pour you out a blessing, that there shall not be room enough to receive it.

–Malachi 3:8-10

Tithes need to be brought into the store house. A store house is where you store your food and go eat. A church, a ministry, or a person that ministers the word to you is your store house. It is where you are fed. It is where your life and family is being impacted and transformed.

You must learn to primarily give where you are fed. If you go eat at Rich's restaurant, you need to pay at Rich's, not Peter's. If you eat at KFC, you should not pay at Olive Garden. When someone ministers in your life and God uses them to bless you, impact your life and make a difference in your life, you need to communicate with them financially (Galatians 6:6). It's like going to a restaurant. You pay for what you get. You don't just go in–sit, eat, and leave.

If Andrew Wommack Ministries has touched your life, if Andrew has blessed you through the ministry and teaching of God's Word, I believe it's appropriate, reasonable, and right for you to give back to his ministry financially.

Should the tithes be given to the local church? I believe tithes should be given to a good local church, not a dead one that is not ministering the Word and changing lives. If your local church is not doing this, you should not continue to give your tithes there. You should take your tithes and give them where you are fed as the number one place to give–where you are being ministered to and edified. On the other hand, offering I believe should be given to ministers, ministries or para-church organizations, benevolent giving, compassionate giving, missionaries support, child sex slavery rescue, orphanages feeding the hungry, those in need, etc.

Chapter Five

Matthew 22:21; Matthew 23:23

"Woe unto you, scribes and Pharisees, hypocrites! for ye pay tithe of mint and anise and cummin, and have omitted the weightier matters of the law, judgment, mercy, and faith: these ought ye to have done, and not to leave the other undone."

—Matthew 23:23

Notice that Jesus did not condemn the Pharisees for paying the tithe. If it were wrong, He would have told them. He instead addressed their hypocrisy.

"They say unto him, Caesar's. Then saith he unto them, Render therefore unto Caesar the things which are Caesar's; and unto God the things that are God's."

—Matthew 22:21

If we understand the spiritual benefit of giving, then we also understand that tithing is not wrong. We should give to God the things that are God's on every level of life, not just in finances. Our prospering is not limited only to the tithe, nor are we cursed if we don't tithe. We are free to enter this grace of God of giving and receiving as much as we want.

Rather than teaching against tithing, we should teach the power and benefit to giving. Giving in many ways benefits the giver more than the receiver. Fruit abounds to our account when we give and partner with the gospel. Philippians 4:17 *Not because I desire a gift: but I desire fruit that may abound to your account.* Luke 6:38 *Give, and it shall be given unto you; good measure, pressed down, and shaken together, and running over, shall men give into your bosom. For with the same measure that ye mete withal it shall be measured to you again.*

Trust the Lord with all thine heart......

Proverbs 3:5-10 *Trust in the LORD with all thine heart; and lean not unto thine own understanding. 6 In all thy ways acknowledge him, and he shall direct thy paths. 7 Be not wise in thine own eyes: fear the LORD, and depart from evil. 8 It shall be health to thy navel, and marrow to thy bones. 9 Honour the LORD with thy substance,* and with the firstfruits of all thine increase: 10 So shall thy barns be filled with plenty, and thy presses shall burst out with new wine.*

These passages are used often to speak of trusting the Lord in many other areas, but one missed area which is what the context is talking about is the area of finances. Although we should trust the Lord across the board and this principle of trusting the Lord can work in other areas, these passages are speaking about trusting God in finances.

We need to trust the Lord with all our heart when it comes to finances, and we should not lean on our own understanding. Honoring the Lord with our finances is proof that we are trusting Him.

Consistent and regular giving

1 Corinthians 16:2 *Upon the first day of the week let every one of you lay by him in store, as God hath prospered him, that there be no gatherings when I come.*

Paul encouraged the Corinthians to be intentional on setting a side on a regular basis as the Lord has prospered them. This was to allow them to be consistent givers, not spasmodic givers. When we give, we need to be consistent. A consistent farmer is more prosperous and blessed than a seasonal farmer. We need to give consistently, not sporadically.

Communicate

Galatians 6:6 *Let him that is taught in the word communicate unto him that teacheth in all good things.*

Communication is more than just words. Giving is a form of communication. When we give, we communicate to a person that we value and appreciate what they have shared and done in our lives. Paul made this point while speaking about the Philippians. They communicated to him through their giving. Philippians 4:14-16 *Notwithstanding ye have well done, that ye did communicate with my affliction. 15 Now ye Philippians know also, that in the beginning of the*

Chapter Five

gospel, when I departed from Macedonia, no church communicated with me as concerning giving and receiving, but ye only. 16 For even in Thessalonica ye sent once and again unto my necessity.

A. Can one tithe in faith?

    a) We should give according to our faith. It is not wrong to tithe-in faith (Romans 14:1-8)

    b) Making a decision to tithe is a matter of faith. Stepping out in faith to support the local church and the work of God is something that God has ordained and something that we cannot afford to neglect. Acts 20:35 says, "…It is more blessed to give than to receive."

    c) Why give or tithe?

        i) It's an act of our love toward the Lord. Love gives. (John 3:16; 1 John 3:18)

        ii) It's an act of worship. (Matthew 2:1, 11)

        iii) It supports the ministers and the work of the ministry. (Deuteronomy 8:18; Malachi 3:10; 1 Corinthians 9:13-14)

        iv) Giving and tithing releases and activates God's power of provision and increase. (Luke 6:38; Genesis 26:12-13)

        v) Growth in faith. Giving money causes a person to grow in the area of trusting God. Learning to give causes us to learn and grow in faith to trust God for anything else we need. (Luke 16:10)

        vi) Meeting the needs of others. (Ephesians 4:28) Giving makes a difference in the lives of others.

        vii) Magnifies and causes others to give thanks to God. (2 Corinthians 9:11-12) Giving invokes gratitude and thankfulness to the Lord.

viii) The principle of sowing and reaping. When we give, there is a promise for a harvest. Although our motive should not be only to get, we can and should expect to receive a harvest only if we have planted (Galatians 6:7-9). When I plant seed in the ground. I do not do that to try the land or test it. I do that to get a harvest.

ix) It demonstrates our trust in the Lord. (Proverbs 3:5, 9)

x) Giving makes us dependent on God and helps us focus on Him as our source. (1 Chronicles 29:10-16)

xi) Giving benefits the giver. (Proverbs 11:24-25) It is an opportunity for an individual to get blessed. "Not because I desire a gift: but I desire fruit that may abound to your account." –Philippians 4:17. When you give, you are not giving up anything. Actually, you are opening the door of blessing from God, and you are going to see fruit released in your life. You are saying, "God, I have put You first and I trust You. The truth is God will take care of you more than you could ever take care of yourself on purpose. You can't out give God.

xii) Giving to God. We should give because we are giving to God not to man.

xiii) Giving honors the Lord. (Proverbs 3:9)

xiv) Giving softens and sensitizes our heart toward the Lord. As a general principle, when we obey the Lord, our hearts get softened and sensitive to Him.

xv) Giving opens doors unto us causing all grace to abound unto us. (2 Corinthians 9:6-10)

B. Abraham and Melchizedek

a) *"And Melchizedek king of Salem brought forth bread and wine: and he was the priest of the most high God. And he blessed him, and said, blessed be*

Chapter Five

Abram of the most high God, possessor of heaven and earth: And blessed be the most high God, which hath delivered thine enemies into thy hand. And he gave him tithes of all." –Genesis 14:18 - 20

   i) Abraham is a picture of the church (Galatians 3:16,19). The promise of Abraham and the blessing of God pronounced on him is for the church.

   ii) Melchizedek is a picture of Christ (Hebrews 7:3 says, *"Without father, without mother, without descent, having neither beginning of days, nor end of life; but made like unto the Son of God; abideth a priest continually."*)

   iii) So, Abraham (a type of the church) gave tithes to the Lord in Melchizedek.

   iv) We tithe because we have been blessed, not to be blessed.

   - Melchizedek blessed Abraham first (Genesis 14:19) before Abraham gave him a tithe (Genesis 14:20). Abraham's tithe was a response to and an acknowledgment of receiving the blessing.
   - Actually, Abraham had been earlier blessed by God (Genesis 12:2-3).

b) Melchizedek still receives tithes.

   i) This shows that tithing is still a principle of promise today because Melchizedek was "made like unto the Son of God" (Jesus Christ)– Hebrews 7:3, still receives tithes (Hebrews 7:8-10).

Net or gross income?

I will end by asking this question that you could be thinking about. Do I tithe on gross or net? Here is a simple principle that I can share with you. Can you tithe on what's not yours? No, you can't. You can only tithe on what is yours.

Truth be said, the gross is not all yours. It includes what belongs to the government. After the government tax deductions, you then have what is truly yours and you should tithe on that. This means you tithe on your net income—which is what is truly yours. This should not be contentious. It's not a command from the Lord (1 Corinthians 11:16). You can still tithe on the gross if you choose or are led by the Lord to do so, but this doesn't make you superior to one who tithes on the net. A dear friend told me that he tithes on his gross because he wants to give to God first—put God first, not the government. He believes that giving on the net is putting God last and government first. This is fine because it works for him—simply his choice. It's simply a personal choice not a doctrine or command from the Lord—as long as you are a cheerful, not tearful giver.

Giving and receiving

Philippians 4:15—"*... no church communicated with me as concerning giving and receiveing but ye only.*"

Notice how Paul uses two words—giving and receiving. Some of us are good givers, but we are poor receivers. We need to humble ourselves to receive if we give. It's fine to harvest or believe for a harvest if you planted seed. It's not inappropriate to expect a harvest if you planted seed.

A farmer does not plant recklessly without an expectation of a harvest and when the harvest time comes, a farmer must harvest and put in the sickle (Mark 4:29). If we are good sowers, we should be equally good reapers. Sowing is not superior to harvesting. They are both important. Paul makes it clear that giving is not complete without receiving—hence, giving and receiving (Philippians 4:15). Not only was Paul given to, he also received.

As a minister of the Word, it's wrong not to receive offerings/tithes. As we encourage people to give, we need to remind them that giving is good for them—which is why we should not shy away from receiving offerings because it benefits the giver even more. Fruit abounds unto their account (Philippians 4:17).

Many have opposed the tithes for many reasons, one of the reasons they claim is that it was strictly an Old Testament principle, but that is not the whole

Chapter Five

truth. We see this tithing principle operating before the law, during, and after the law. I pray that this chapter helps shed light on the area of tithe and offerings.

Chapter Six

How Can I Know God's Will?

Anytime we are talking about God's will, we are talking about God's heart, desire, passion, and delight. The best way to find out God's will on any subject is to go into His Word. His Word is His will. God has clearly spelled out His will through His written Word. We can't look for God's will elsewhere without His Word.

Unlike what some think, God's will has been fully laid out in the Bible. We are going to examine some of the areas that God's general will is spelled out clearly in Scripture. The heart of us knowing God's will is to follow it and fulfill it. God's will is not followed and fulfilled automatically.

Everyone who gets to know the Lord is driven to know His will with a desire to follow it. God has clearly revealed His will in Scripture, so we should be more focused on that than anything else. Before we get God's specific will for our lives, we must first do our best to adhere to the written will of God clearly spelled out in Scripture.

First, God's will is to "BE." The Scriptures clearly show us that we ought to "BE" and after BEING God's will, we will DO God's will. BEING precedes DOING God's will. If we can't "BE" God's will, we can't DO it! God's will has to be understood in terms of being, not just doing, going, or having. As we "be" God's will, our character is built and developed to a place where we can do it. God's will is not something we *do,* but first, something we must *be.*

The Word says, Therefore:

- Be born again (John 3:3)
- Be holy and godly (Titus 2:11-12)
- Be filled with the Holy Ghost (Ephesians 5:14-19)
- Be thankful (1 Thessalonians 5:18)
- Be separate (2 Corinthians 6:17)
- Be transformed by the renewing of your mind (Romans 12:1-2)
- Be a light to the world and salt of the earth (Matthew 5:13-16)
- Be a blessing (Genesis 12:2)
- Be merciful and kind to one another. (Ephesians 4:32)
- Be a witness (Acts 1:8)
- Be fruitful and filled with the knowledge of His will (Colossians 1:9-12).

Once we have settled the part of being God's will, we can then move on to the doing. This makes the doing easier.

"Jesus saith unto them, My meat is to do the will of him that sent me, and to finish his work."

—John 4:34

There are two main categories of God's will:

a) General will of God for all people

God gives His general will for us in every area—spiritually and naturally. This is laid out in His written Word (Psalm 119:105). Knowing God's Word is equivalent to knowing His will. Knowing His will is impossible without knowing His Word. It all starts with knowing His written Word. If we disobey in the general guidance/God's will as clearly laid out in the Word, we will hinder ourselves from receiving the specific will or guidance. In this chapter, I will be sharing in detail what entails the general will of God.

"I beseech you therefore, brethren, by the mercies of God, that ye present your bodies a living sacrifice, holy, acceptable unto God, which is your reasonable service. And be not conformed to this world: but be ye transformed by the

renewing of your mind, that ye may prove what is that good, and acceptable, and perfect, will of God."

–Romans 12:1-2

This passage clearly shows the process we need to take to prove or manifest the will of God. That main step is renewing our minds. We need to get in the Word and change the way we think from the ways of the world to the ways of the Kingdom of God.

b) Specific will for each individual

After we are submitted to God's general will, the Holy Spirit then leads us to God's specific will for our lives. This specific will never contradicts or opposes the general will of God. To the degree we are submitted and aligned to God's general will is the degree to which we will be led into His specific will for our lives.

2 Thess. 3:10 tells us to **work**, but it doesn't say where to work or what kind of work, but it is the Holy Spirit who tells us what kind of work we are to do and where. This is specific guidance.

Another example is marriage. The Word of God (general guidance) encourages us to marry and teaches us to marry only the opposite sex. However, it doesn't tell us to marry anyone or who to marry specifically apart from the general guidance that we should marry a believer in the Lord (2 Corinthians 6:14). It is the Holy Spirit who gives us those specifics–who to marry and when.

God's general will in detail

a) Salvation to all mankind

"The Lord is not slack concerning his promise, as some men count slackness; but is longsuffering to us-ward, not willing that any should perish, but that all should come to repentance."

–2 Peter 3:9

GOT QUESTIONS?

"Who will have all men to be saved, and to come unto the knowledge of the truth."

—1 Timothy 2:4

God's general will is that not any person perish. God is not willing that people be lost, which is the reason He sent Jesus to die for the sins of the whole world. As we know, some will perish, not because God wills it, but because they chose to reject God's offer of salvation. They used their free will to choose otherwise.

"Grace be to you and peace from God the Father, and from our Lord Jesus Christ, Who gave himself for our sins, that he might deliver us from this present evil world, according to the will of God and our Father:"

—Galatians 1:3-4

b) Godly and righteous living, denying ungodliness and worldly lusts

"For the grace of God that bringeth salvation hath appeared to all men, Teaching us that, denying ungodliness and worldly lusts, we should live soberly, righteously, and godly, in this present world; Looking for that blessed hope, and the glorious appearing of the great God and our Saviour Jesus Christ; Who gave himself for us, that he might redeem us from all iniquity, and purify unto himself a peculiar people, zealous of good works."

—Titus 2:11-14

God's will for us all is to live godly and righteously in this present world. God's general will teaches that we should deny ungodliness and worldly lusts. If we aren't doing this, we are not in God's general will and this could hinder us from receiving God's specific will.

c) Healing

"And, behold, there came a leper and worshipped him, saying, Lord, if thou wilt, thou canst make me clean. And Jesus put forth his hand, and touched him, saying, I will; be thou clean. And immediately his leprosy was cleansed."

—Matthew 8:2-3

Chapter Six

Notice the words "I will." This man questioned the willingness of Jesus, and He confirmed that it was His will to heal. Healing is God's will. Jesus' answer reflects His will. God would not be willing to do that which is not His will. God only does His will.

d) Abstain from fornication

"For this is the will of God, even your sanctification, that ye should abstain from fornication: That every one of you should know how to possess his vessel in sanctification and honour; Not in the lust of concupiscence, even as the Gentiles which know not God: That no man go beyond and defraud his brother in any matter: because that the Lord is the avenger of all such, as we also have forewarned you and testified. For God hath not called us unto uncleanness, but unto holiness."

–1 Thessalonians 4:3-7

Many want to know God's will for their lives, but they are not following this general will that is clearly laid out in the Word. God's will is for us to be consecrated (separated and set apart for pure and holy living) so that we can abstain from fornication. This is God's will. The word "fornication" was translated from a Greek word, porneia, which means "harlotry, incest, idolatry and adultery". This is the same word from which we get the word "pornography." Those who are living ungodly lifestyles are not living according to God's will. God has called us to live a godly life and abstain from all the sexual perversion and filth. If we are not sanctifying ourselves, abstaining from fornication and possessing our bodies unto sanctification and honor, we are not in God's will.

The word "abstain" means *to refrain, hold oneself off* (Strong's Concordance). It is staying away, keeping away, turning away, but mainly to run away from or to flee from. (1 Corinthians 6:8 and 1 Thessalonians 4:4-5)

If we can avoid all kinds, forms, and appearance of evil, we can abstain from it. Avoiding is key to refraining. We can't successfully and continuously refrain from what we do not avoid. This is a choice you must make. No one can make it for you. We must choose to abstain from evil and all the appearance of it.

Some people foolishly think they are very strong, or very mature, and they go as close as possible to sin as they can, and they eventually yield to it. We should not flirt with sin. That is not removing ourselves from it. Toying with sin is not a good idea. Those who toy and flirt with it will fall to it soon or later. This is clearly not abstaining.

Like all evil, fornication has an appearance. We need to flee fornication and its appearance. One of the reasons we fall into sin is because we neglect all the warning signs and refuse to stay away or depart from all appearance of evil.

We should make all efforts to avoid evil. We should foresee it and hide. (Proverbs 22:3) Our natural tendency is not to depart, abstain or flee from evil. It takes effort and it must be done deliberately. Do not put yourself in compromising and tempting situations - remove yourself.

e) Thanksgiving

"In every thing give thanks: for this is the will of God in Christ Jesus concerning you."

–1 Thessalonians 5:18

Giving thanks is the will of God. Being unthankful is acting against God's will for our lives. We thank God in the midst of everything we are going through because He is a good God and will deliver us.

Everything is not the will of God. Notice also that this passage of Scripture says that we are to give thanks **IN** everything, not **FOR** everything. Some people have read "for" everything rather than "in" everything, and it has changed the entire meaning of this verse.

Chapter Six

God is not the One behind the bad things that happen to us. We should not be thanking Him for bad things and evil. He has nothing to do with it. For everything the devil has done, God has done something good. Romans 8:28 *"And we know that all things work together for good to them that love God, to them who are the called according to his purpose."*

f) To be filled with the Holy Spirit.

"Wherefore be ye not unwise but understanding what the will of the Lord is. And be not drunk with wine, wherein is excess; but be filled with the Spirit;"

–Ephesians 5:17-18

Rather than being drunk with wine, this passage makes it clear that it is God's will for us to be filled with the Holy Spirit. This denotes a continued action. I believe one of the reasons for us to be continuously filled with the Holy Spirit is because in our souls, we are leaky vessels.

g) Employer and employee

"Servants, be obedient to them that are your masters according to the flesh, with fear and trembling, in singleness of your heart, as unto Christ; Not with eye service, as men pleasers; but as the servants of Christ, doing the will of God from the heart; With good will doing service, as to the Lord, and not to men: Knowing that whatsoever good thing any man doeth, the same shall he receive of the Lord, whether he be bond or free."

–Ephesians 6:5-8

These passages reveal that it is God's will for us to serve our masters (employers and bosses) specifically in respect and reverence in singleness or sincerity of heart, as unto Christ not unto men, not with eye service as men pleasers do.

If we do our work as unto men and not as unto the Lord, we are not doing God's will. This speaks of motives of the heart. We should not do what we do to be seen of men.

h) Subject to authority

> *"Submit yourselves to every ordinance of man for the Lord's sake: whether it be to the king, as supreme; Or unto governors, as unto them that are sent by him for the punishment of evildoers, and for the praise of them that do well. For so is the will of God, that with well doing ye may put to silence the ignorance of foolish men: As free, and not using your liberty for a cloke of maliciousness, but as the servants of God."*
>
> –1 Peter 2:13-16

God's will is for us to submit to authority. This is not speaking about obedience, but rather submission. Submission is not synonymous to obedience. For one, submission is more of an attitude than action, although submission in many cases leads to an action. On the other hand, obedience is more of an action than an attitude. It is possible to do the right thing but have a wrong attitude. This act of being subject to authority will cause others to see our well-doing and silence the ignorance of foolish men.

> *"Epaphras, who is one of you, a servant of Christ, saluteth you, always laboring fervently for you in prayers, that ye may stand perfect and complete in all the will of God."*
>
> –Colossians 4:12

Chapter Seven

What about Healing?

No one wants to be sick. When a man gets sick, he will do anything to get healed. Good health and healing is a universal need. In this chapter, I would like to discuss four fundamental truths about healing and walking in supernatural health.

A. Sickness and disease is a result of sin, Satan and the fall of man

All sickness started in the garden of Eden at the fall of man. Sin entered into the world and with it brought sickness, diseases, death, misery, pain, sorrow and so forth.

Had man not disobeyed God in the garden, sin wouldn't be here, nor would diseases and sickness. Satan, the author of sin, now uses sickness and disease to afflict people. *Genesis 2:15-17 says, "And the LORD God took the man, and put him into the garden of Eden to dress it and to keep it. And the LORD God commanded the man, saying, Of every tree of the garden thou mayest freely eat: But of the tree of the knowledge of good and evil, thou shalt not eat of it: for in the day that thou eatest thereof thou shalt surely die."*

God had nothing to do with sin, death, or sickness. We should never blame Him for what man, Satan, and sin have caused (John 10:10). The creation story clearly shows that God created only good and not evil.

a) *"He that committeth sin is of the devil; for the devil sinneth from the beginning. For this purpose the Son of God was manifested, that he might destroy the works of the devil."* –1 John 3:8

b) *"The thief cometh not, but for to steal, and to kill, and to destroy: I am come that they might have life, and that they might have it more abundantly."* – John 10:10

c) *"How God anointed Jesus of Nazareth with the Holy Ghost and with power: who went about doing good, and healing all that were* **oppressed of the devil***; for God was with him."* –Acts 10:38 (Emphasis mine).

d) *"And ought not this woman, being a daughter of Abraham, whom* **Satan hath bound***, lo, these eighteen years, be loosed from this bond on the Sabbath day?"* –Luke 13:16 (Emphasis mine).

B. It's God's will to heal–all the time

Jesus would never have done that which is not God's will. He always perfectly performed God's will. The fact that Jesus healed the sick should settle any doubts as to whether is it God's will to heal because He came to do God's will (Hebrews 10;7 and John 6:38). Everything that Jesus did was God's will. That includes healing.

Our will also has a part in healing. Will we take that which God wills for us? When our will meets God's will, we get the results for which we are believing.

a) *"And Jesus, moved with compassion, put forth his hand, and touched him, and saith unto him, I will; be thou clean."* –Mark 1:41

Healing is God's will. God willed to heal this man and He healed him. One of the reasons He willed to heal him was also because He loved this man. Because God loves us so much, He always wills to heal us and made the full provision for that healing to occur.

i) Hebrews 13:8 says that Jesus is the same yesterday, today and forever. This shows that if He did it before, He will do it today.

Chapter Seven

    ii) *"Is any sick among you? let him call for the elders of the church; and let them pray over him, anointing him with oil in the name of the Lord: And the prayer of faith shall save the sick, and the Lord shall raise him up; and if he has committed sins, they shall be forgiven him."* –James 5:14-15

b) He healed them all

    i) *"Now when the sun was setting, all they that had any sick with divers diseases brought them unto him; and he laid his hands on **every one of them, and healed them**."* –Luke 4:40 (Emphasis mine).

    ii) *"And when the men of that place had knowledge of him, they sent out into all that country round about, and brought unto him all that were diseased; And besought him that they might only touch the hem of his garment: **and as many as touched were made perfectly whole**."* –Matthew 14:35-36 (Emphasis mine).

    iii) *"But when Jesus knew it, he withdrew himself from thence: and great multitudes followed him, and **he healed them all**;"* –Matthew 12:15 (Emphasis mine).

    iv) *"And the whole multitude sought to touch him: for there went virtue out of him, and **healed them all**."* - Luke 6:19 (Emphasis mine).

c) *"And said, If thou wilt diligently hearken to the voice of the LORD thy God, and wilt do that which is right in his sight, and wilt give ear to his commandments, and keep all his statutes, I will put none of these diseases upon thee, which I have brought upon the Egyptians: for am the LORD that healeth thee."* –Exodus 15:26.

    i) The Lord spoke this to over 3 million Israelites.

    ii) God is a healing God. "I am the Lord that healeth thee."

d) *"Who forgiveth all thine iniquities; who healeth all thy diseases;"* –Psalm 103:3.

- i) God heals ALL our diseases.
- ii) God forgives ALL our iniquities

e) *"Beloved, I wish above all things that thou mayest prosper and be in health, even as thy soul prospereth."* –3 John 1:2.

- i) Good health is God's will. He desires His children to walk in wholeness—spirit, soul, and body. The same price that paid for our sin also paid for our healing. Every part of us (Spirit, Soul, and Body) has been bought at a price, so we should glorify God in all, not just in one (1 Corinthians 6:20).

C. Healing is a part of our redemption

Most people believe that Jesus died for their sins, but still struggle with the truth that He also paid for their healing, deliverance, and prosperity. Salvation was not just a provision for only one thing. It was a full package that included healing among others. You can't separate the forgiveness of sins from healing. Jesus paid for it all. Jesus bore our sins and our sickness. He is the healing Savior.

a) The word "SAVE or SAVED", as used in the New Testament, it is a Greek word sózō, which means more than forgiveness of sins but also physical healing, deliverance, prosperity, protection and being made whole. So, we see that healing was a part of the redemption that Jesus paid for at Calvary. Jesus wants you well the same way He wants you born again.

- i) The Greek word *sózō* is used in Romans 10:9, 13 as well as James 5:15.

b) Healing and forgiveness of sins are mentioned together.

Healing and the forgiveness of sins were purchased together and should be offered together. It's all one package. It's God's will to forgive sins as is His will to heal us.

Chapter Seven

i) *"Surely he hath borne our griefs, and carried our sorrows: yet we did esteem him stricken, smitten of God, and afflicted."* –Isaiah 53:4.

ii) *"When the even was come, they brought unto him many that were possessed with devils: and he cast out the spirits with his word, and healed all that were sick: That it might be fulfilled which was spoken by Isaiah the prophet, saying, Himself took our infirmities, and bare our sicknesses."* –Matthew 8:16-17

- This verse says that Isaiah 53:5 was being fulfilled by Jesus. Jesus had just healed people physically.
- Matthew substituted *"griefs"* and *"sorrows"* for *"infirmities and sickness"* which further proves that Isaiah 53 is talking about our physical healing.

iii) *"Who his own self bare our sins in his own body on the tree, that we, being dead to sins, should live unto righteousness: by whose stripes ye were healed."* –1 Peter 2:24.

- The word healed is talking about being cured, made well and whole.

iv) *"Whether is easier, to say, Thy sins be forgiven thee; or to say, Rise up and walk? But that ye may know that the Son of man hath power upon earth to forgive sins, (he said unto the sick of the palsy,) I say unto thee, Arise, and take up thy couch, and go into thine house."* –Luke 5:23-24.

- Notice that Jesus offered forgiveness of sins and healing to this man together at the same time. It also shows that healing is part of the atonement.

D. Healing requires faith to be received

In receiving healing, just as in receiving forgiveness of sins, we have a part to play. That part is faith. We must believe God in order to receive. Faith is the key that releases our healing and forgiveness of sins.

GOT QUESTIONS?

Grace is what God does for us, but faith is our response to God's grace. Grace provides the food, faith cooks it. God doesn't give us grace and then turn around and believe for us. We must step out in faith to receive the things of God. This is how the kingdom works.

Faith is expecting and trusting God to do what He has promised in His Word. When God gives us a promise in His Word, that promise creates faith, which produces action. Everything God asks us to believe, He has promised to do. Real faith is taking God at His Word and stepping out upon His promise with all confidence and sincerity, without doubt or fear.

The main difference between those who receive and those that don't is faith.

a) *"And he said unto her, Daughter, thy faith hath made thee whole; go in peace, and be whole of thy plague. While he yet spake, there came from the ruler of the synagogue's house certain which said, Thy daughter is dead: why troublest thou the Master any further? As soon as Jesus heard the word that was spoken, he saith unto the ruler of the synagogue, Be not afraid, only believe."* –Mark 5:34-36

b) *"Jesus said unto him, If thou canst believe, all things are possible to him that believeth."* –Mark 9:23

c) *"And when he was come into the house, the blind men came to him: and Jesus saith unto them, Believe ye that I am able to do this? They said unto him, Yea, Lord. Then touched he their eyes, saying, According to your faith be it unto you."* – Matthew 9:28-29

d) *"For unto us was the Gospel preached, as well as unto them: but the word preached did not profit them, not being mixed with faith in them that heard it."* –Hebrews 4:2

   i) Faith is required to profit from healing. Faith comes by hearing God's Word,

Chapter Seven

e) *"But let him ask in faith, nothing wavering. For he that wavereth is like a wave of the sea driven with the wind and tossed." –*James 1:6

   i) Faith that wavers not is the faith that will receive. When we ask, it must be done in faith without wavering.

   ii) We do not need big faith, what is needed is faith as small as a mustard seed, but it must not be contaminated or polluted by unbelief.

Chapter Eight

"I thought I was healed, but I'm sick again. What happened to my healing?"

Most people have been healed and have received physical healing, or have seen someone healed of some sort of thing or disease, but in some situations find that the very same sickness or symptoms returned. There are several reasons why this could happen, and in this chapter we will discuss these.

One possibility is because of a counterattack from the devil. We can be tempted to think that once we are healed, there is nothing else we need to do. I beg to differ. I actually believe there is a lot more to do. It's our responsibility to keep the switch turned on and not let anyone walk in and turn the lights off.

It is possible to be healed and yet fall sick again, and so because of this, some have turned against God. God supplied the healing, but Satan doesn't want you healed and he will fight to see you fall sick again. This is spiritual warfare, not vacation. There are certain things that we can do to ensure that we do not lose or allow the previous sickness to return.

God's word is clear that Satan is the one responsible for stealing, killing and destroying (John 10:10). It's not God who does all these things to His children. God is not guilty, nor has he ever been. That is a wrong picture of God. God is a good God and Satan is a bad devil. Period. God wants you well, Satan wants you sick (Acts 10:38).

GOT QUESTIONS?

A. Matthew 12:43-45

"When the unclean spirit is gone out of a man, he walketh through dry places, seeking rest, and findeth none. Then he saith, I will return into my house from whence I came out; and when he is come, he findeth it empty, swept, and garnished. Then goeth he, and taketh with himself seven other spirits more wicked than himself, and they enter in and dwell there: and the last state of that man is worse than the first. Even so shall it be also unto this wicked generation."

a) The unclean spirit is one who causes sickness and disease.

b) When this spirit is cast out of a man (healing happens).

c) This spirit goes around looking for a new place of rest (1 Peter 5:8) and when it can't find one, it returns to its previous residence.

d) Notice that this spirit refers to your body as its "house" (1 Corinthians 6:19-20).

e) "When he comes". Notice the use of the word "when". It didn't say IF, but WHEN. This is saying that Satan will try to return. It's just a matter of time.

f) Jesus clearly warns us that there will be a counterattack from Satan after the demon is cast out or after we receive our healing, which will be even worse than the previous experience. The verses clearly say that the evil spirit will go and take seven more spirits or sicknesses that are fiercer than its self.

g) We should not stay empty. We need to protect our house (body) that was inhabited by the devil and fill it such that when it returns, there will be no room for it to dwell. Your body which was its former "house" will no longer be its house.

This is not to say that we should be believing for the devil's counterattack, or living in fear, but we must take certain steps to stop it from ever

Chapter Eight

happening again. Our faith is not to be exercised for what is evil or wrong.

The enemy will come back knocking on your door ("his house") and if its empty, he will seek to enter again.

B. James 4:7

"Submit yourselves therefore to God. Resist the devil, and he will flee from you."

a) Submit to God

If you do not submit to God, you might as well forget resisting the devil. If you are on the same side as the devil, you can't fight him or resist him. It just won't work. So, the first step to ensuring that you retain your healing is to submit to God.

b) Resist the Devil

The word *"resist"* here is not a onetime thing that we do and then turn on our TV and watch "as our stomach turns". This word *"resist"* denotes an active, continuous act. This is not talking about being passive. Your passiveness gives the devil opportunities to destroy you.

It is saying we must continuously, and actively fight against the devil. I know it is bad news for those of you who wanted to do totally nothing. One of the things that you want to do to continue to walk in the healing you received and good health thereafter is to continuously resist the enemy. Matthew 11:12 "…*the kingdom of heaven suffereth violence, and the violent take it by force."*

One of the prominent figures of modern Christianity who saw many people healed was Smith Wigglesworth. He was famous for not playing around with the devil. He got angry at Satan.

We need to get angry at what I call the **S³** (Satan, sin, and sickness) and all the evil Satan is doing to us and others. The truth is you can't truly fight against that which you do not hate. Ephesians 4:26-27 *"Be ye angry, and sin not: let not the sun go down upon your wrath: Neither give place to the devil."*

When we resist the devil, what are we resisting? We have to resist all the works of the devil such as stealing, killing, destruction, sickness, disease, sin, poverty, on and on the list goes.

If you start having any symptoms of what you experienced before, you don't sit there and do nothing. You should speak back to those symptoms (Mark 11:14) that are speaking to you and command them to leave in Jesus' name. You must do something. Speak the word (promises of God), rebuke them in Jesus' name and say no to those symptoms or whatever sickness or disease that is trying to return. Do not agree with or tolerate those pains or symptoms, however insignificant they may feel to you. If you give the devil an inch, rest assured, he will take a mile. This is what resisting the devil looks like.

Feeling vs. believing

Do not let your feelings lead your decision-making. Stand on God's promises no matter how you feel. For instance, we may occasionally have doubts as to whether we are saved but we do not let those feelings and thoughts rule because we are assured of what the word says. However, when it comes to healing, when we experience those very similar thoughts and feelings in our physical body, we immediately discard or forget what we believe and what the word teaches about healing. Why is it? We should stand firm in our healing even as we do in our salvation (forgiveness of sins).

Although the devil has been defeated, he is not dead. He is still going about as a roaring lion seeking whom he may devour (1 Peter 5:8 and John 10:10).

Chapter Eight

C. God's Word

"Then said Jesus to those Jews which believed on him, If ye continue in my word, then are ye my disciples indeed; And ye shall know the truth, and the truth shall make you free."

–John 8:31-32.

The other thing we can do that I believe is the best is to fill ourselves with the word of God. We must study God's word and be so grounded in it that we can't be shaken by an attack of the enemy. It is the best weapon against the enemy and his tools such as sickness and disease (Ephesians 6:17, Hebrews 4:12). We must know it and believe it.

One reason people cannot keep their healing, or that sickness keeps lingering around their doorstep, is because they do not know the word of God. They are dependent on someone else to tell them what it teaches and says. They are not disciples of Jesus. Such are susceptible to various attacks and counterattacks from the enemy and the result is a loss of their healing.

People receive healing through the gifts of the Spirit, not only through the word. You can go and receive through someone who operates in the supernatural gifts of healing and miracles. There is a place for the supernatural gifts of miracles and healing. However, you do not keep your healing by the gifts of the Spirit (working of miracles, the gifts of healing etc.). You can receive it by the gifts, but you can't keep it by the gifts. You keep it by maturing in the knowledge and revelation of the word of God and faith. Begin to study and grow in God's word. This is the best means and the most consistent. We must learn to be healed based on God's word more than the gifts of the Spirit operating in another person's life. Again, the best way to receive and retain healing is through the word of God that we feed ourselves and grow in–not through the gifts of the Spirit (1 Corinthians 12:8-12). I'm not diminishing the gifts of the Spirit, but I'm saying that the best way is for us to learn and receive directly through the Word.

Continuous freedom doesn't come by the gifts of the Spirit, but directly by and through the word of God and the revelation of His word to you. You can't live your life off the gifts of the Spirit. You must graduate to a place where you know God's word for yourself and you can draw and receive healing from it by yourself, one-on-one with the Holy Spirit. God designed us to live life on nothing else but God's word (Matthew 4:4). Do you know God's word? Do you know His promises to you concerning healing? Do you know His will for you? What healing verses are you standing on? Uh, how many?

In your case, there may have been a miraculous shortcut to a supernatural healing–praise the Lord! I'm for it all day, but please understand that this does not mean that there will not be a counterattack from Satan. There is effort required on your part to continue to walk in healing. We walk by faith every day of our lives (Romans 1:17; Galatians 3:11). We never go on a vacation from faith because it is a part of us. Our faith itself is from God (Galatians 2:16). We must step out in faith concerning healing just as we do concerning receiving salvation. There is no exception to walking in or using faith.

God's word is the seed that we must plant into our hearts, watering it with faith to the point that when a counterattack from the enemy comes, we can stand and resist.

Talked out of your healing

Some people who were once healed were talked out of their healing, so they lost what God had done in their lives. They allowed the enemy to come in and steal the word (Mark 4:15-17). Because of a lack of maturity and depth into God's word, they were deceived by someone and what they had was gone. If you have been healed of anything before, you will realize that not everyone is happy about it. This underscores the need to study God's word and move on to become mature disciples, not just babes or converts. Babes and converts are the greatest prey for the enemy. Study and grow in the area of healing that you have received. This will help you minimize or stop any counterattacks. Do not get mad at the preacher. Do not get mad at God. Get mad at the real thief, Satan, and take back your healing. You can still be healed again. Do not give up hope. After you

Chapter Eight

receive your healing, move on and hide God's word in your heart, renew your mind (Romans 12:1-2) and keep what God has given or done for you. If Satan can steal the word out of your heart, he can steal your miracle or healing.

D. Change of Doctrine

    Sometimes we start off believing the right thing but end up in the weeds believing the wrong thing. If you change what you believe about healing to something false, rest assured that the devil will come in and counterattack easily. You will lose your healing or something else will come on you. You do not want that.

    We must continue in the teachings of healing, grace, faith and so forth. For example, if you quit believing that it is God's will to heal us all the time, how will you retain your healing? We can't be tossed to and fro by every wind of doctrine and expect to walk in the victory. We need to continue in the word (John 8:31-32) and get grounded even deeper. Wrong teaching = wrong believing = wrong results.

E. Change of lifestyle

"Know ye not, that to whom ye yield yourselves servants to obey, his servants ye are to whom ye obey; whether of sin unto death, or of obedience unto righteousness?"

–Romans 6:16.

a) The way we live our lives speaks to who we are truly yielded and submitted to.

"Submit yourselves therefore to God. Resist the devil, and he will flee from you."

–James 4:7

    Certain lifestyles such as homosexuality, adultery, and fornication to name a few, are lifestyles that attract the devil into our lives. Living this way is not submitting to God and it takes away our high ground of resisting the devil. How do you resist that which you are submitted to? Some lifestyles invite certain sicknesses back. We must watch the way we live, lest we let the devil back into our lives.

In John 5, Jesus healed a man at the pool of Bethesda. When he found the man later in the temple, He told him to "Behold, thou art made whole: sin no more, lest a worse thing come unto thee. (John 5:14).

Jesus was not prophesying doom, but was warning the man to change his way of life. If we do not change, we will be a target of the enemy and could be attacked by sickness or other problems.

F. Still attacked

Sometimes you have done all that you know to do, but for some reason, you lose your healing. This is possible, but the way to fight back is the same. Take the word of God, resist the devil, check what you believe, check your lifestyle.

It's time to get your guns out, not because you are believing for the thief to break in, but to be ready to fire just in case he breaks in. Do the training required to keep yourself sharp, alert and to master your weapon so that if a counter attack ever comes, you can run the devil and his demon midgets off. Your body is no longer Satan's house as before (Matthew 12:44). It's no longer empty, but filled with the power, presence of God and the word of God. There is no room for the devil. You have been equipped by the Lord to overcome the devil at every turn.

Finally, if you ever get healed by the gifts of the Spirit (healings, miracles, etc.), continue or start to study and mature in the word of God. Renew your mind and prepare yourself to fight back should the devil ever come back knocking on your door.

G. Learn to keep what you get

Everything you get you must learn how to keep. It is kept by faith and the word of God. We can lose what we have received from the Lord (John 5: 14). Therefore, the best form of deliverance and healing is through

Chapter Eight

the word of God inside a person, not through the gifts of healing of another person. The Word is health to all our flesh (Proverbs 4:22). You can still go and receive from someone with the supernatural gifts of healing and miracles in operation. There is a place for the supernatural gifts of miracles and healing.

It is important to go by what you believe, not by what you see, smell or feel in the natural realm, however, ignoring the physical is not faith. In Mark 8:22-25, Jesus did not ignore the physical problems but instead responded in faith. Every time we respond to a situation, it should be in faith. Jesus responded again to a situation the second time in this man, but in faith, not in doubt. Jesus was not praying (petitioning) for this man the second time to cause healing to occur that hadn't occurred yet. He was just adding another dose of His power in faith. He was not praying once more to move God, but to move the devil! Do not give up because something has not manifested or "worked out" the first time.

In conclusion, I want to recommend a book called **"Your Healing Door"** by Pastor Greg Mohr. This book will help you. It is excellent.

Chapter Nine

Is it God's Will to Heal Me?

No one can study the Bible without twisting it and conclude that it's not God's will to heal. God's fingerprints on healing are all over His Word. It's so plain that you can't miss it if you don't want to. Disease and sickness are the will of Satan, not God. Some believe and teach that God heals, but not all the time. This is not true.

*"And Jesus went about all Galilee, teaching in their synagogues, and **preaching** the Gospel of the kingdom, and **healing** all manner of sickness and all manner of disease among the people."* (Emphasis mine).

–Matthew 4:23

Jesus always did God's will. The fact that Jesus healed the sick should settle any doubts as to whether it is God's will to heal. He came to do God's will (Hebrews 10:7 and John 6:38) and everything that Jesus did was God's will, which included healing.

Our will also has a part in the question of healing. Will we take that which God wills for us? When our will meets God's will, the work gets done–healing manifests.

If you do not believe (Romans 10:9-10) you cannot be born again, but also if you do not believe that it is God's will to heal, you will not be healed (Mark

6:5-6). Your free will can hinder His will for you. To see healing, you need to align your will with His will, which is to heal. Healing starts with believing that it is God's will to heal people all the time. This is foundational. It is the starting place to receiving healing. Once this is settled, then faith will come (Romans 10:17), and healing will manifest.

A. Power of God was to heal

> *"And it came to pass on a certain day, as he was teaching, that there were Pharisees and doctors of the law sitting by, which were come out of every town of Galilee, and Judea, and Jerusalem: and the power of the Lord was present to heal them."*
>
> –Luke 5:17

    a) Notice that the word *"present"* is in italics, which means it was added to make the sentence grammatically correct. But the way this is in the original language is "….God's power is to heal."

    b) God's power is not just present to heal occasionally. His *power is to heal* and is always present. If it weren't His will, this would not be true.

B. I will

God's will is fully revealed through Jesus.

> *"And Jesus, moved with compassion, put forth his hand, and touched him, and saith unto him, I will; be thou clean."*
>
> –Mark 1:41

    a) Healing is God's will. God willed to heal this man and Jesus healed him. God wills healing because it is His will. If healing was not His will, He would have responded "I will not" rather than "I will."

    b) Hebrews 13:8 says that Jesus is the same yesterday, today and forever.

        i) This means that if He did it before, He will do it today.

Chapter Nine

c) *"Is any sick among you? let him call for the elders of the church; and let them pray over him, anointing him with oil in the name of the Lord: And the prayer of faith shall save the sick, and the Lord shall raise him up; and if he has committed sins, they shall be forgiven him."* –James 5:14-15

Although it is good to try to convince people that they are believing wrongly about things, it makes no sense to argue with a person's will. It's their will and it will always prevail. They have a right to their will. We all have wills. Some are spoken, some are unspoken, some written and some unwritten. If someone had a will, you have to know what it is for you to know the heart and the desire of that person.

In this case, God's will is His written Word. When we read the will of Jesus (His Word), we see His will to heal in His Word and actions with people.

a) Healing starts with believing that it is God's will to heal people all the time. His actions and His written Word prove that.

b) Anyone who doesn't come to this conclusion and thereby believe that God wants him well will never receive healing for themselves.

c) *"Jesus Christ the same yesterday, and today, and for ever."* –Hebrews 13:8

d) If Jesus did not do the Father's will, which includes healing, then the kingdom of God would be divided; and therefore, would not stand. *"And if a kingdom be divided against itself, that kingdom cannot stand. And if a house be divided against itself, that house cannot stand."* (Mark 3:24-25).

If God did it in the Old Testament and in the New Testament, and He is the same yesterday, today and forever, it still remains God's will to heal us all today.

C. Jesus came to do God's will

a) The Scriptures are very clear, and Jesus said over and over that He came to do God's will. God's will includes forgiveness of sins, healing, protection, provision and setting the captives free. Everything Jesus did was the will of God. If you want to see the will of God, look at Jesus' actions and words.

b) *Then said I, Lo, I come (in the volume of the book it is written of me) to do thy will, O God."* –Hebrews 10:7

   i) Notice that Jesus said that He came to do the will of God the Father.

c) *"For I came down from heaven, not to do mine own will, but the will of him that sent me."* –John 6:38

   i) Jesus was sent by God the Father and all that He did was His will.

d) *"And there was delivered unto him the book of the prophet Esaias. And when he had opened the book, he found the place where it was written, The Spirit of the Lord is upon me, because he hath anointed me to preach the Gospel to the poor; he hath sent me to heal the brokenhearted, to preach deliverance to the captives, and recovering of sight to the blind, to set at liberty them that are bruised, To preach the acceptable year of the Lord."* –Luke 4:17-19

D. New Testament

Various Scriptures in the New Testament reveal that it is God's will to heal all the time.

a) *"That it might be fulfilled which was spoken by Esaias the prophet, saying, Himself took our infirmities, and bare our sicknesses."* –Matthew 8:17

   i) This verse was quoted as a fulfillment of Isaiah 53:5 in reference to the healing that Jesus had done in Matthew 8:16 where He healed them all. *"But he was wounded for our transgressions, he was bruised for our iniquities: the chastisement of our peace was upon him; and with his stripes we are healed."*

   ii) Matthew substituted *"griefs"* and *"sorrows"* for *"infirmities and sickness"* which further proves that Isaiah 53 is talking about our physical healing.

Chapter Nine

      iii) You have the right to forgiveness of sins as well as healing, according to Isaiah 53:4-5 and Matthew 8:17, if you believe.

  b) *"How God anointed Jesus of Nazareth with the Holy Ghost and with power: who went about doing good, and healing all that were oppressed of the devil; for God was with him."* –Acts 10:38

      i) This is how Peter summarized the life and ministry of Jesus.

      ii) He healed all, not a few.

      iii) Healing is a good work.

      iv) People are oppressed by the devil, NOT God.

  c) *"And besought him that they might only touch the hem of his garment: and as many as touched were made perfectly whole."* –Matthew 14:36

      i) As many as touched were made perfectly well.

          ○ God wants you perfectly well, not just well.

      ii) Because it is God's will to heal, as many as touched Him were made perfectly well. Again, this would have never happened if it weren't God's will.

      iii) *"And the whole multitude sought to touch him: for there went virtue out of him and healed them all."* –Luke 6:19

      iv) *"Now when the sun was setting, all they that had any sick with divers diseases brought them unto him; and he laid his hands on every one of them, and healed them."* –Luke 4:40

      v) *"Beloved, I wish above all things that thou mayest prosper and be in health, even as thy soul prospereth."* –3 John 1:2

E. He healed them all

If healing is for all, salvation is for all, and if salvation is for all, definitely healing is for all.

a) *"Now when the sun was setting, all they that had any sick with divers diseases brought them unto him; and he laid his hands on **every one of them, and healed them**."* –Luke 4:40 (emphasis mine).

b) *"And when the men of that place had knowledge of him, they sent out into all that country round about, and brought unto him all that were diseased; And besought him that they might only touch the hem of his garment: **and as many as touched were made perfectly whole**."* –Matthew 14:35-36 (emphasis mine)

c) *"But when Jesus knew it, he withdrew himself from thence: and great multitudes followed him, and **he healed them all**;"* –Matthew 12:15 (emphasis mine)

d) *"And the whole multitude sought to touch him: for there went virtue out of him, and **healed them all**."* –Luke 6:19 (emphasis mine).

    i) The Lord would not have healed them ALL if it was not His will. By Jesus healing all the people, it shows that it is His will to heal.

F. Old Testament

Healing is not only a New Testament reality, but also an Old Testament reality. If God would heal people under the inferior covenant (OT), how much more those under the superior covenant (NT), (Hebrews 7:22; 8:6-7).

a) *"And said, If thou wilt diligently hearken to the voice of the Lord thy God, and wilt do that which is right in his sight, and wilt give ear to his commandments, and keep all his statutes, I will put none of these diseases upon thee, which I have brought upon the Egyptians: for I am the Lord that healeth thee."* –Exodus 15:26

    i) The Lord spoke this to over three million Israelites.

    ii) God is a healing God. "I am the Lord that healeth thee."

    iii) God promised to heal the children of Israel and also described

Chapter Nine

Himself as the Lord who heals them. The Lord would not describe Himself inaccurately. If He said it, then it is true and it shows that it is His will to heal.

    iv) God is a healer by nature. Healing is His default position. If it was not God's will to heal, Jesus would and could never have done it. He represented the Father perfectly by doing His will. It would have been a sin for Jesus not to heal because it was already settled that it was God's will.

b) *"And ye shall serve the Lord your God, and he shall bless thy bread, and thy water; and I will take sickness away from the midst of thee. There shall nothing cast their young, nor be barren, in thy land: the number of thy days I will fulfil."* –Exodus 23:25-26.

c) *"He sent his word, and healed them, and delivered them from their destructions."* –Psalm 107:20

    i) God would not have sent His word to do that which is not His will. This verse further proves that healing is God's will.

d) *"Bless the Lord, O my soul, and forget not all his benefits: Who forgiveth all thine iniquities; who healeth all thy diseases; Who redeemeth thy life from destruction; who crowneth thee with lovingkindness and tender mercies; Who satisfieth thy mouth with good things; so that thy youth is renewed like the eagle's."* –Psalm 103:2-5

    i) Part of our benefits and package as children of God is healing. This is not to say that God does not give healing to unbelievers–He does.

    ii) God forgives all our iniquities and heals all our diseases. This is God's will to heal us all the time. If it's God's will to forgive our sins, it's equally His will to heal our diseases.

    iii) God heals ALL our diseases.

        iv) God forgives ALL our iniquities

e) *"And the LORD will take away from thee all sickness, and will put none of the evil diseases of Egypt, which thou knowest, upon thee; but will lay them upon all them that hate thee."* –Deuteronomy 7:15

    i) Notice that it says God WILL take away.

        ○ First, it is God's will to remove ALL sicknesses from us.

    ii) God takes away sickness and disease from His children. He does not take life as Job believed (Job 1:21), especially under the New Covenant and the dispensation of grace.

G. Prosper and be in good health

"Beloved, I wish above all things that thou mayest prosper and be in health, even as thy soul prospereth."

–3 John 1:2

a) Good health is God's will. He desires His children to walk in wholeness–spirit, soul, and body. The same price that paid for our sin also paid for our healing. Our spirit and body have been bought with a price and therefore we should glorify God in all, not in just one. (1 Corinthians 6:20)

b) God desires you to be in good health. He wants your physical body to be healthy just as He desires your spiritual and soulish realms to be healthy.

It is God's will for each person to be not only healed of disease and sickness, but to walk in supernatural health. He created our bodies with a self-healing capability which further reveals that it is His will to heal. If you will believe His Word, you will begin to see the benefits of this promise.

Chapter Ten

What Does God Hate?

"These six things doth the Lord **hate: yea, seven are an abomination unto him: A proud look, a lying tongue, and hands that shed innocent blood, An heart that** *deviseth wicked imaginations, feet that be swift in running to mischief, A false witness that speaketh lies, and he that soweth discord among brethren."*

–Proverbs 6:16-19

Most people would be shocked to find out that God hates. They think you should never hate under any circumstances. They think hate is of the devil. Although hate could be used in a wrong or negative way, it can also be used in a positive way. I believe hate becomes bad when it is directed toward people. It should not be toward people. We live in a fallen world where there are so many things looking to destroy our lives. We can't just get along and love the very things that are trying to get rid of us and are detrimental to our survival. Contrary to what many people believe, *God is a hater.* They think hate is not of God; however, there are certain things that He hates, and we need to teach people of what He hates. Some things we love in are the very antithesis of what God loves. I'm a hater, just like my Father–What He hates I hate!

If we never hate anything, we would never be able to make a difference in this world. Some people discover a passion and take on entire careers dedicated to stopping the very things they hate. I just can't understand how a police officer, for example, can do his job and yet not hate the evil he sees, or tries to stop. He need to hate that evil for him to be effective and a good police officer.

The hatred we are talking about is a Godly hatred that hates sin and evil, but loves the sinner. God sent Jesus to die for the ungodly (sinner). If He hated them–God forbid, He would not have died for them. God is a lover of people who all sinned. He hastes sin and the damage such as hurt, sickness, diseases, pain, lack, sufferings it brought to mankind as a whole.

Hate is a missing ingredient in our lives that is costing us a lot. It is time to hate again and it's time to stir up the hate in us. God has given us the ability to hate and we should use it. He loves people, but hates sin and evil because of the hurt and damage it does to us, but above all because He loves us and wants the best for us.

No man on earth was as loving as Jesus, yet we see that Jesus was a hater–a hater of iniquity. Hebrew 1:9 says *"Thou hast loved righteousness, and hated iniquity; therefore God, even thy God, hath anointed thee with the oil of gladness above thy fellows."* Jesus hated iniquity and wickedness. A true disciple of Jesus Christ must hate iniquity. Some people just need to learn how to hate, and many things in their lives will change for the better. One of the problems we experience today is because we have not stirred up our hatred toward evil in our days.

We have all heard the saying that love is blind. I beg to differ. Blind to what? If blind, then definitely not blind to evil. True love hates what is evil (Psalm 97:10). Why would someone not have hatred for sickness which is out to take their lives? One of the reasons many people have not been healed is because they don't hate sickness. Although they do not necessarily love it, a lack of hatred for it is a reason it is still hanging around; otherwise, you would have done something to stop it because you hate it so much.

The evil and ungodliness you don't hate and resist can and will kill you. *"Submit yourselves therefore to God. Resist the devil, and he will flee from you."* (James 4:7)

The word "abomination" means "something *disgusting* (morally), that is, (as noun) an *abhorrence;*" (Strong's Concordance).

Chapter Ten

A. Proud look

   a) Contrary to our present culture, God hates arrogance and pride.

   Proverbs 13:10 says that only by pride comes contention. The root at the heart of the problems we face is pride and self-centeredness.

   b) Because you kick a ball (Soccer pro) or throw a ball (basketball pro), that is no reason to be caught up in pride.

   - Your looks, qualifications, eloquence, education, wealth, background is no reason to have pride in our hearts.

   c) If we have our self-worth and identity wrapped in what we do rather than who we are, we will be caught up in pride.

B. Lying tongue (deception, holding back information or leaving the wrong impression). All lying originates from Satan, the father of lies. (Proverbs 12:19; John 8:44)

C. Hands that shed innocent blood

   a) This is talking about murder, not killing. Murders–unjustified killings are abhorred by the Lord. There are justified killings. For example, killing an animal for food is not wrong, so is self-defense and justified wars.

   God hates the killing of babies in the womb. This is true innocent blood. We should hate abortion because it is murdering the innocent child in the mother's womb. God hates abortion.

   - If you do not hate what God hates, you need to either get born again, spirit filled, or renew your mind.

   "I've noticed that everyone who is for abortion is already born"

   –President Ronald Reagan.

GOT QUESTIONS?

b) Infanticide

   i) Infanticide is the evil, ungodly act crime of killing an infant or a child within a year of birth, especially one who has survived the act of abortion.

   ii) Evil is publicly promoted in our society. If our leaders hated evil and ungodliness, *Planned Parenthood* would have been out of business decades ago.

I came across a news article by The Great Rush Limbaugh that detailed how the US congress voted on an anti-infaticide bill. In February 2019, Senator Ben Sasse of Nebraska proposed a simple bill in the United States Senate. It's called the Born-Alive Abortion Survivors Protection Act (S. 311). It had one objective—to force lawmakers to go on the record about whether they support or oppose infanticide.

The summary of the bill by Ben Sasse read along these lines, If an abortion results in the live birth of an infant, the infant is a legal person for all purposes under the laws of the United States and the Constitution, and is entitled to all the protections of such laws.

What were the results? The bill failed because it was opposed. The final vote was 53 to 44. They needed 60 votes for the bill to pass. Several Democrat candidates for the Democratic presidential nomination in 2020 (Sens. Cory Booker (N.J.), Sherrod Brown (Ohio), Kirsten Gillibrand (N.Y.), Kamala Harris (Calif.), Amy Klobuchar (Minn.), Jeff Merkley (Ore.) and Elizabeth Warren (Mass.)–plus independent Sen. Bernie Sanders (Vt.)–voted against the Born-Alive Abortion Survivors Protection Act.

All democrats apart from three (Democratic Sens. Bob Casey (Pa.), Doug Jones (Ala.) and Joe Manchin (W.Va.) voted in favor of this bill. All the rest of the democrats voted to block (against) the bill. In other words, they voted for infanticide.

Chapter Ten

D. Heart that deviseth wicked imaginations

    a) *"A heart that manufactures wicked thoughts and plans, feet that are swift in running to evil,"* –Proverbs 6:18 (AMP).

    b) This is speaking about imagining, manufacturing, thinking, planning, plotting, conniving wicked, ungodly things, and evil.

        i) God not only hates evil, but He also hates the imagining and planning of it. People are only concerned with the outside actions of people, but God sees right through to the heart of man. He is disgusted by the evil and wicked thoughts and plans of our hearts toward evil.

        ii) *"The thought of foolishness is sin: and the scorner is an abomination to men."*–Proverbs 24:9

E. Feet that be swift in running to mischief

    a) "Mischief" is referring to evil.

        i) God hates swiftness to evil.

        ii) Some people love sin and will do anything to sin–quickly. We all sin, but we all don't run swiftly to it. We should be very slow to sin, but that starts with a hatred for it.

    b) If we had a hatred for evil, we would not be swift going into it.

    For example: Hollywood and the work they do speaks volumes of what evil is. The junk they pump through the TV sets is despicable. It has corrupted and destroyed many people's lives, marriages, children, youth, and so forth in the name of "entertainment". This is not entertainment, but *enterpainment* (It brings pain). I can't stand the demonic, ungodly, nasty, so-called "hip-hop" filthy rap, the sexually arousing and violent music culture and I will not pay for it. I do not pay for what I hate!

Garbage in, garbage out! Some have paid big bucks for this worldly sewage and junk to come into their homes through television which have been the very things that have destroyed their lives.

c) We live in a world where people are no longer shy nor ashamed of evil and sin. They publicly do the despicable on live TV such as late-night shows while many are busy applauding.

   i) In the past adultery was never celebrated however, today, people pay big money for sin and the promotion of evil. We should be shunning evil not embracing it.

I remember a guy in Uganda who was celebrated for having sex live on TV. People came out on the streets and were celebrating a "hero", yet he was a zero with the rim knocked off. This was like a celebration of Absalom who had sex publicly with the father's wives (2 Samuel 16:20-22). The spirit of Absalom is being celebrated by many today. What a shame!

The many people we call **celebrities** are **sillybrities** in my humble opinion. They promote evil. The sexual perversion we see today is partially because of us not having this hatred for iniquity, not people or sinner (Hebrews 1:9; Psalm 97:10). Look at the negative impact it has brought to our society.

F. False witness that speaketh lies

   a) It's one thing to lie, but it's another thing to deceptively witness against a person. Character assassination is abhorred by God. Lying against a person is so bad that it could sometime cost another person's life. God hates it. (John 8:44; Proverbs 12:19)

   b) Justice Brett Kavanaugh and Neil Gorsuch hearings are two examples to look at as relates to false witnesses. Today, if you do not like someone, just lie about it and everyone will pretty much run with it.

      i) "And the judges shall make diligent inquisition: and, behold, if the witness be a false witness, and hath testified falsely against his

Chapter Ten

brother; Then shall ye do unto him, as he had thought to have done unto his brother: so shalt thou put the evil away from among you. And those which remain shall hear, and fear, and shall henceforth commit no more any such evil among you."–Deuteronomy 19:18-20

G. Soweth discord among brethren

   a) The Lord hates the six things above, but he really hates sowing discord and strife. Such a person that sows discord among brethren brings division among brethren and goes against the unity that the Lord loves. James 3:16 tells us the dangers of strife is confusion and every evil work.

This is all a godly kind of hatred that hates sin and evil, but loves the sinner. Our lives will change proportional to what we hate and love. As we shall see later, true love has certain things it will hate. If you love something, you will equally havet to hate another to keep and protect what you love.

One of the reasons we fall into such sins is because we do not hate them. If we treated sin like a snake that needs to be killed and not turned into a pet, we would do a lot better. We must treat these things like a plague they are. Sin is a plague, and we must hate it and fight it. The first step to beating sin is to be born again (John 3:3), then renewing of the mind (Romans 12:1-2). Accepting Jesus into our hearts as our Lord and Savior is the beginning of this hatred for sin and evil. When we get saved, we receive a brand new heart that loves righteousness and hates iniquity (Hebrews 1:9). We also get a new spirit that empowers us to live victoriously in this life. The only antidote for sin and evil is Jesus–not the law.

It's what we learn to hate that we will not allow near us. Take a look at King David and the effects of his sin. He brought tremendous misery to his entire life because of a lack of hatred for adultery and murder. This lack of hate for the sin and evil came back to sting him. I truly believe that David could not have easily fallen for Bathsheba had he had a fear of the Lord and hatred for evil, ungodliness, and sin. **What he didn't hate but allowed, he committed!** David paid heavily. His infant son died. His son, Absalom, committed treason against him. Absalom killed his brother Ammon. Ammon committed incest with his sister. Absalom had sex publicly with David's wives. David became a vagabond running for his life. He lost his kingdom and suffered shame and dishonor.

Jesus hated iniquity

Hebrew 1:9 says *"Thou hast loved righteousness, and hated iniquity; therefore God, even thy God, hath anointed thee with the oil of gladness above thy fellows."*

a) Jesus hated and hates iniquity and lawlessness, so should we. Hating iniquity is a Godly thing.

   i) A true disciple of Jesus Christ must hate iniquity.

b) Would you say you love righteousness? Then you MUST hate iniquity if you love righteousness. Genuine love hates–it hates what is evil and ungodly (Psalm 97:10).

   i) Those who claim to love righteousness but do not hate iniquity are deceived, ignorant, or not born again.

c) Jesus was evelaed to destroy the works of the devil (1 John 3:8). These works are stealing, killing, and destroying. They are evil, ungodly and lawless.

   ◦ Jesus would not have destroyed the works of the devil if He did not hate them. You can't destroy what you do not hate.

Love the sinner, hate the sin

Thou shalt not hate thy brother in thine heart: *thou shalt in any wise rebuke thy neighbor, and not suffer sin upon him.* (emphasis mine)

— Leviticus 19:17

"These six things doth the L<small>ORD</small> hate: *yea, seven are an abomination unto him: A proud look, a lying tongue, and hands that shed innocent blood, An heart that deviseth wicked imaginations, feet that be swift in running to mischief, A false*

Chapter Ten

witness that speaketh lies, and he that soweth discord among brethren." (emphasis mine)

– Proverbs 6:16-19

a) The first verse makes it clear not to hate thy brother.

b) The second verse tells us that God hates things, not people.

> You need to separate the sinner from the sin, the act from the actor. We are never instructed to hate the sinner. We have to be careful not to hate the sinner in the attempt to hate iniquity, evil, and sin thinking the sinner is one with their sin. If we do not separate their sin from them, they will be unreacheable and we won't be willing to reach out and help them. The hate we are talking about becomes bad when it is directed toward people. It should not be toward people, but sin.

a) Jesus loves the sinner, but hates sin, iniquity, and evil. He **loves the actor, not the act. He was the best example of hating evil, yet He never hated the sinner**. He came to die for sinners, because He loved us, not hated us. How do you know that Jesus loves you? Well, He died for you. He would not have done that if He didn't.

  i) No man on earth was as loving as Jesus, yet we see that Jesus was a hater–a hater of iniquity.

  ii) People have written books trying to assure you that God hates you because of the way you are living or what you did in the past. Nothing could be further from the truth.

   ○ What you did was foolish, but that did not stop Him from loving you. He still loved you and wants to help you. He hates sin and evil because it is detrimental to you. Sin hurts us.

   ○ God is not your enemy. He is not against you. He is against evil and sin that brings damage.

b) God's love will never leave a person the same. It will bring Him to repentance. (Romans 2:4)

c) Some people will want you to love them and also condone their sin. Loving the sinner does not mean condoning sin or evil and ungodliness nor does it mean you should never deal with the sinner.

   i) It is not because you hate the sinner, but hate the sin. Sometimes you can hardly separate the sinner from the sin, and you have to deal with both (Proverbs 13:10), but even in such a situation you do not do something to them, but for them. For instance, I would fire a person for something they have done such as lying and stealing yet, I do not hate them. I did that for them, not to them. In truth, they fired themselves. They disqualified themselves. I just enforced their decision of departing.

d) We must speak the truth to the sinner. If we do not, we aren't walking in love toward them.

   i) The woman at the well (John 4:7-42)

   ii) The woman caught in the act of adultery (John 8:3-11)

One time I was entering a grocery store, and I saw a bunch of guys stealing products that were on display at the entrance of the supermarket. Because I hated evil, I called the security on them and we ran after them to apprehend them. If I did not have a fear of the Lord, I wouldn't have done that. I hated what they were doing, but I did not them, but to also stop what they were doing, I had to pursue them.

Not only does God hate evil, but He has given us the same ability and has instructed us to hate evil. The verses below speak volumes about hatred–hatred of evil.

a) ***"Ye that love the LORD, hate evil:*** *he preserveth the souls of his saints; he delivereth them out of the hand of the wicked."* –Psalm 97:10 (emphasis mine)

Chapter Ten

    i) Hating evil and loving the Lord go hand in hand. Those who hate evil love the Lord. This shows that hating is a good thing, if we are hating evil.

b) *"The fear of the LORD is to hate evil: pride, and arrogance, and the evil way, and the froward mouth, do I hate."* –Proverbs 8:13

    i) According to this verse, the true fear of the Lord is to hate evil. In case you missed it the first time in Proverbs 6, this passage repeats it.

        o God hates pride, arrogance, the evil way, and the froward mouth. The Lord hates these things.

        o Anyone who claims to have the fear of the Lord but does not hate evil is lying or lacks revelation.

    ii) God spoke what He hates. We need to speak out loud what we hate. For instance, "I hate adultery and I love faithfulness."

        o Life and death are in the power of the tongue. We need to speak out loud what we hate and what we love. If we love something, then we have to hate something else to complete our love for whatever we say we love.

    iii) *"By mercy and truth iniquity is purged: and by the fear of the LORD men depart from evil."*–Proverbs 16:6

        o Fear of the Lord = Hate evil (Provers 8:13) = depart from evil (Proverbs 16:6)

    iv) To depart from evil, we have to hate it. We can't overcome or depart from what we do not hate. As long as we are still in love with certain things, we can't overcome them.

        o One of the deterrents from sin is to develop a hatred for it. Very few people will do what they hate.

We won't depart from what we do not hate. We need to work on our capacity to hate evil. If you do not hate evil, sin, and ungodliness, you will participate in it like King David.

- c) *"Let love be without dissimulation. Abhor that which is evil; cleave to that which is good."* –Romans 12:9
    - i) This verse tells us to hate evil and cleave unto that which is good. One of the ways we hate evil is by cleaving to that which is good.
    - ii) Genuine love has a hatred for evil. This kind of love is without hypocrisy. When we hate evil, we cleave to what is good.
        - ○ We can't cleave to what is good if we do not hate evil.
    - iii) Sickness and disease are evil. We need hatred for disease and sickness
        - ○ One of the reasons many people have not been healed is because they don't hate sickness. Although they do not love it, a lack of hatred for it is a reason it is still hanging around otherwise you would have done something to stop it because you hate it so much.
        - ○ If you are believing God for healing, you need to hate evil, sickness, and disease.
    - iv) Poverty is evil. It is not good. Do not love poverty. We need hatred for poverty. Poverty came to steal, kill, and destroy.
- d) *"There was a man in the land of Uz, whose name was Job; and that man was perfect and upright, and one that feared God, and eschewed evil."* –Job 1:1
    - i) This text says that Job eschewed evil, which means he abstained or shunned evil." Just as we can't depart from something we do not hate, we won't truly abstain from something we do not hate because when we hate something, we lose the desire to participate in it.

Chapter Ten

    ii) Shunning evil leads to abstaining and departing from it.

e) *"Be ye angry, and sin not: let not the sun go down upon your wrath: Neither give place to the devil."* –Ephesians 4:26-27

    i) *"Submit yourselves therefore to God. Resist the devil (resist evil), and he will flee from you."* –James 4:7 (parentheses mine)

- You can't resist what you do not hate.

    ii) Be angry at sin.

- Jesus was angry at sin and made a whip and drove merchants out of the temple. He did this twice at the beginning and at the end of His ministry.
- John 2:14-17; Matthew 21:12-16; Mark 11:15-18; Luke 19:45-46

    iii) **"Stand in awe, and sin not:** *commune with your own heart upon your bed, and be still. Selah."* –Psalm 4:4 (emphasis mine)

- The word "awe" here means to be angry (see the NKJV, and the Amplified Bible). This is talking about a godly anger as Ephesians 4:26-27.
- If we aren't angry, we will sin, allow evil, iniquity and ungodliness. Anger is meant to fight against sin and evil and its author–Satan.

f) *"Woe unto them that call evil good, and good evil; that put darkness for light, and light for darkness; that put bitter for sweet, and sweet for bitter!"* –Isaiah 5:20

    i) As long as we do not develop or practice a hatred for evil and sin, we will end up calling evil good, and good evil. If we hate evil, we won't make the mistake of calling good evil and evil good.

g) *"Seek good, and not evil, that ye may live: and so the Lord, the God of hosts, shall be with you, as ye have spoken.* **Hate the evil, and love the good**, *and* **establish judgment** *in the gate: it may be that the Lord God of hosts* *will be gracious unto the remnant of Joseph."* —Amos 5:14-15 (emphasis mine)

- i) These two verses instruct us to not only hate evil, but to also love the good. If we do, then we will establish judgment. A lack of hatred for evil and love for good will result in a lack of judgement.
    - Hating evil = fearing God = loving the good
- ii) Many people do not have a fear of the Lord because of their love for the things of this world. We cannot love the world and love God at the same time. It's impossible. We need to choose one and give up on the other.
    - *"Love not the world, neither the things that are in the world. If any man love the world, the love of the Father is not in him. For all that is in the world, the lust of the flesh, and the lust of the eyes, and the pride of life, is not of the Father, but is of the world."* —1 John 2:15-16
    - World is refering to the things and ways of the world that is contrary to the Word of God—*the lust of the flesh, and the lust of the eyes, and the pride of life.*

h) *"By mercy and truth iniquity is purged: and by the fear of the Lord men depart from evil."* —Proverbs 16:6

- i) The true fear of the Lord results in departing from evil. Anyone who claims to love the Lord and does not depart from evil is lying.
  i) *"He deviseth mischief upon his bed; he setteth himself in a way that is not good; he abhorreth not evil."* —Psalm 36:4
- i) We need to abhor (hate) evil lest we devise mischief and set ourselves in a way that is not right.

j) *"I hate and abhor lying: but thy law do I love."* —Psalm 119:163

Chapter Ten

i) Here, the Psalmist tells us that he hated and detested lying but loved the Word of God. Loving the Word of God will produce hatred for sin and lying. Those who do not know nor love the Word of God have no hatred for sin and the ungodliness that is going on in our society. If we truly hated ungodliness, we would never entertain ourselves with the perverted movies that we bring into our homes. If people would fall in love with the Word of God, they would naturally develop a hatred for sin and ungodliness. No love for the Word = no hatred for sin and ungodliness (A lot of what we see as a hatred for evil is skin deep and selfish at the core).

ii) According to Proverbs 8:13 and Proverbs 16:6, the fear of the Lord is defined as to depart from evil, but we can't truly depart from evil unless we hate it. Therefore, to depart from evil is to hate it. We can't overcome what we do not hate. As long as we are still in love with certain things, we can't overcome them. Hate is one of the ways to depart from evil and sin. No hatred, no departing. In the same breath, we can't resist what we do not hate (James 4:7). If you don't hate the devil and his works such as stealing, killing and destroying, you won't resist him effectively.

God's heart is clear. He loves people. He loves the sinners, but He hates sin and everything it brings with it. His hating of sin is to our benefit.

Chapter Eleven

How is Christianity Different from all Other Religions?

All religions have one thing in common: they are searching for God (even if they don't call Him God, or they think there may be many gods and goddesses). They do this in a multitude of ways, but they are all trying to find God and gain His favor by their sacrifices and good deeds.

Christianity is different. Instead of us searching for God, God is searching for us! Instead of us reaching up to God, God is reaching down to us! God became a man and lived among us for the purpose of redeeming us all (Philippians 2:5-11 and 1 Timothy 3:16). This is why Jesus (who is God Almighty) is so important, because He came down from heaven to do for us what we could never do for ourselves: bring us to God. We could not save ourselves nor cleanse ourselves from sin. Man is helpless. It took God to become a man to do this. God is perfect and holy, and we are separated from Him by our sins (Romans 3:23 and Isaiah 59:1-2). No matter how hard we try, we cannot erase the stain or scar of sin by ourselves, but by His death and resurrection, Christ did this for us.

1. Jesus Christ

    a) The Lord Jesus Christ is the center and foundation of the Christian faith, and He is also the reason Christianity differs from all the other religions that people follow.

GOT QUESTIONS?

    b) Although you will find some "Christian" denominations that claim to be Christians, they are not, and do not believe or hold foundational what the Scriptures teach about Jesus. Examples: Jehovah witness, Mormons, Jesuits and many more.

    c) If any group does not hold to the foundational Scriptures teaching about Jesus such as His virgin birth, deity, sinless life, death and resurrection, they cannot be Christian.

        i) **Jesus did not come to bring a religion, but a relationship with God.**

2. The Resurrection

"In the end of the sabbath, as it began to dawn toward the first day of the week, came Mary Magdalene and the other Mary to see the sepulcher. And, behold, there was a great earthquake: for the angel of the Lord descended from heaven, and came and rolled back the stone from the door, and sat upon it. His countenance was like lightning, and his raiment white as snow: And for fear of him the keepers did shake, and became as dead men. And the angel answered and said unto the women, Fear not ye: for I know that ye seek Jesus, which was crucified. He is not here: for he is risen, as he said. Come, see the place where the Lord lay. And go quickly, and tell his disciples that he is risen from the dead; and, behold, he goeth before you into Galilee; there shall ye see him: lo, I have told you. And they departed quickly from the sepulcher with fear and great joy; and did run to bring his disciples word. And as they went to tell his disciples, behold, Jesus met them, saying, All hail. And they came and held him by the feet, and worshiped him."

—Matthew 28:1-9

    a) These two women looked, but did not see a body. He was gone—RISEN, indeed. Jesus is alive! God is NOT dead. Hallelujah!

    b) Because He is alive, there is hope for your situation. You can experience life and the resurrection power of God in every area of your life. This

Chapter Eleven

can be your personal life, your health, marriage, business, job, the list goes on and on.

One of the greatest arguments for and proof of Christianity is the resurrection of Jesus. Jesus prophesied His death and then rose again from the dead fulfilling His Word (Matthew 12:40; John 2:18-19). The resurrection is the most crucial aspect of the deity and life of Jesus.

a) Many people who claimed deity such as Mohammed, Buddha, Krishna and many more are still dead, but Jesus rose again from the dead.

b) No other religion or belief system boasts of their leader's resurrection. This is one attribute of Christianity that distinguishes it from any other religion.

c) Anyone with power over death deserves:

   i) Our attention

   ii) Deserves to be heard

d) Jesus was not an average man. He was God. He is God. That is why His death, burial, and resurrection are such a big deal.

Empty tomb

"Paul, an apostle, (not of men, neither by man, but by Jesus Christ, and God the Father, who raised him from the dead.)"

–Galatians 1:1

a) This is the most amazing event in all human history. No other religion has an empty tomb.

b) The enemies of Jesus could have easily stopped all talk of the resurrection by producing His dead, decaying body, but there was no dead body for them to produce! The tomb in which He was buried is empty to date!

GOT QUESTIONS?

"Now the next day, that followed the day of the preparation, the chief priests and Pharisees came together unto Pilate, Saying, Sir, we remember that that deceiver said, while he was yet alive, After three days I will rise again. Command therefore that the sepulcher be made sure until the third day, lest his disciples come by night, and steal him away, and say unto the people, He is risen from the dead: so the last error shall be worse than the first. Pilate said unto them, Ye have a watch: go your way, make it as sure as ye can. So they went, and made the sepulcher sure, sealing the stone, and setting a watch."

–Matthew 27:62-66

a) Some of the reasoning that was given for the absence of Jesus' body was that the disciples had stolen His body. However, to prevent such from happening, the chief priests and Pharisees went to Pilate to have the tomb sealed and guarded by soldiers.

b) On a side note, to their credit, they remembered the prophecies about His resurrection while the believers did not and did all the preparation to stop it.

c) I don't believe any of the disciples were that trained and skillful to take on these armed Roman soldiers. These same men had fled in fear when He was being taken by the soldiers and then crucified.

d) A *"watch"* was a total of four men squad (according to Acts 12:4) and they were fixed and armed at the tomb with a three-hour rotation. Even more, the sealing of this tomb was in such a way that one could tell when the stone was moved because the seal would have been broken. It is said that a clay seal was placed at the tomb of Jesus.

e) The sealing of the tomb is one of the greatest proofs that Jesus resurrected. The Roman soldiers standing guard made sure that no one could steal His body, yet he was resurrected anyway. They were witnesses to the greatest miracle in the history of the world.

"And when they were assembled with the elders, and had taken counsel, they gave large money unto the soldiers, Saying, 'Say ye, His disciples came by night,

Chapter Eleven

and stole him away while we slept. And if this come to the governor's ears, we will persuade him, and secure you.' So they took the money, and did as they were taught: and this saying is commonly reported among the Jews until this day."

—Matthew 28:12-15

- a) The elders and the Pharisees had to plot and lie because they could not explain it away. The Man was risen! Again, their lying shows that Jesus rose from the dead. If He had not risen from the dead, then there would have been no cause to lie and connive about it.

- b) The very men who were put out to guard the tomb were the very ones to witness the greatest event of all history, yet they allowed themselves to be bought out of it.

- c) If Jesus was really a fraud like many religions have said, the disciples would not have allowed themselves to be martyred for a liar. The simple fact is that the resurrection of Jesus cannot be explained away!

A. First to be raised from the dead, and never to die again.

Jesus was not the first one to be raised from the dead. Many other people in Scripture were raised from the dead, but only to die again.

- a) Elijah raised the widow's son from the dead (1 Kings 17:22)

- b) Elisha raised the Shunammite woman's son from the dead (2 Kings 4:35)

- c) A man came back to life after his dead body was thrown and touched the dead bones of Elisha (2 Kings 13:21)

- d) Jesus raised Lazarus (John 11; Matthew 9:25; and Luke 7:15)

- e) Peter raised Dorcus from the dead (Acts 9:40-41)

- f) Paul raised Eutychus from the dead (Acts 20:7-21)

Jesus prophesied His death and resurrection and then rose again from the dead, fulfilling His Word. (Matthew 12:40; John 2:18-19) He prophesied His death and resurrection a total of 14 times (7 public and 7 private). He defeated the grave!

"And he is the head of the body, the church: who is the beginning, the firstborn from the dead; that in all things he might have the preeminence."

–Colossians 1:18

    a) Jesus was the first one to die and resurrect, but NEVER to die again. When Jesus resurrected from the dead, He resurrected with a spiritual body that could never die again.

B. Four parts to the Gospel

"Moreover, brethren, I declare unto you the Gospel which I preached unto you, which also ye have received, and wherein ye stand; By which also ye are saved, if ye keep in memory what I preached unto you, unless ye have believed in vain. For I delivered unto you first of all that which I also received, how that Christ died for our sins according to the scriptures; And that he was buried, and that he rose again the third day according to the scriptures:"

–1 Corinthians 15:1-4

    a) These verses make it clear that the Gospel has four parts to it.

        i) The Christ

        ii) The death for our sins

        iii) The burial

        iv) The resurrection

    b) The Gospel is incomplete without all four of these parts. Jesus the Christ (God), died, was buried, and rose again.

Chapter Eleven

    c) We have to believe the three aspects of the Gospel to be truly born again. We can't believe one and reject another. For instance, if you don't believe that Jesus rose from the dead, you can't be saved even though you believe He died on the cross.

C. "…that God raised Him from the dead…"

"That if thou shalt confess with thy mouth the Lord Jesus, and shalt believe in thine heart that God hath raised him from the dead, thou shalt be saved. For with the heart man believeth unto righteousness; and with the mouth confession is made unto salvation."

– Romans 10:9-10

    a) These verses make it clear that we have to confess with our mouth and believe in our heart that God raised Him from the dead to be saved.

    b) When some people talk or minister to others about salvation, they fail to mention or highlight that the person must believe in Jesus' resurrection to be saved.

        i) Those who do not believe that Jesus rose again from the dead cannot be saved.

    c) Just having someone just repeat a sinner's prayer and not have him confess that he believes that Jesus was raised again from the dead is not a Biblical way to minister salvation.

    d) The word "saved" in the Greek language is *"sozo"* which means safety, to be made whole, deliverance, the forgiveness of sins, healing, protection, and prosperity.

        i) If we want to experience all the above, we need to believe in our hearts that Jesus has been raised from the dead–that He is alive. If Jesus is not alive, there is no hope for the above. There is nothing to receive from a dead God! Jesus is alive. We have hope for everything we need in this life.

D. Jesus was seen by the twelve disciples and by more than 500 others after His resurrection.

> "And that he was seen of Cephas, then of the twelve: After that, he was seen of above five hundred brethren at once; of whom the greater part remain unto this present, but some are fallen asleep."
>
> —1 Corinthians 15:5-6

    a) The evidence supporting the resurrection of Jesus is overwhelming. First, there were over five hundred eyewitnesses of the risen Christ! These are a lot of eyewitnesses. Five hundred voices should not be ignored. This is a powerful detail of the resurrection of Jesus.

    b) Jesus did not rise spiritually, but bodily. A spirit cannot be seen. Jesus was seen by many after His resurrection. Resurrection changed everything.

        i) If Jesus was a phony, He would have said that He will rise from the dead spiritually, hence leaving no evidence for his resurrection, but He said and rose again physically.

        ii) No religion boasts this truth. Even the grave is empty to this day.

E. The resurrection, our hope!

> "Now if Christ be preached that he rose from the dead, how say some among you that there is no resurrection of the dead?"
>
> —1 Corinthians 15:12

    a) The resurrection of the Lord Jesus is proof that there is a resurrection for believers.

F. If Christ is not risen…

> "But if there be no resurrection of the dead, then is Christ not risen: And if Christ be not risen, then is our preaching vain, and your faith is also vain."
>
> —1 Corinthians 15:13-14

Chapter Eleven

a) These verses make it clear that if Christ never rose from the dead, then our preaching and our faith is in vain. In other words, we cannot be born again and we are believing in vain and we are still in our sins.

b) If Jesus did not rise from the dead then all believers who have died have perished having no hope of resurrection, and if this is true, then believers are the most miserable of all men because there is no hope of them ever resurrecting. 1 Corinthians 15:17-19 says, "And if Christ be not raised, your faith is vain; ye are yet in your sins. Then they also which are fallen asleep in Christ are perished. If in this life only we have hope in Christ, we are of all men most miserable."

G. When Jesus won, we won with Him through faith

Every believer in Christ died with Him, was buried with Him, and also was raised with Him. Furthermore, we are seated with Him in heavenly places (Ephesians 2:6) and our life is hid with Him in God. We identified with Jesus in all areas through faith in Him. All these are realities in our Spirit man, but one day in the future, we will experience a bodily resurrection and we will get a new body, never to die again. This body will be immortal, incorruptible and one of flesh and bones. (Luke 24:39)

The word *"resurrection"* is used in reference to the physical body resurrection, while the words *"raised"* and *"rise"* are typically used in reference to our current state in our spirits right now, hence the terms, "risen with Him", "raised with Him." If we believe on Jesus and receive the gift of righteousness He offers, then our spirit has been raised as a result of Jesus' bodily resurrection. (Romans 4:25; Colossians 2:12-13)

a) *"Buried with him in baptism, wherein* **also ye are risen with him through the faith** *of the operation of God, who hath raised him from the dead."* – Colossians 2:12 (emphasis mine)

b) *"If ye then be risen with Christ…" For ye are dead, and your life is hid with Christ in God."* –Colossians 3:1, 3

c) *"But I would not have you to be ignorant, brethren, concerning them which are asleep, that ye sorrow not, even as others which have no hope. For if we believe that Jesus died and rose again, even so them also which sleep in Jesus will God bring with him. For the Lord himself shall descend from heaven with a shout, with the voice of the archangel, and with the trump of God: and the dead in Christ shall rise first."* –1 Thessalonians 4:13-14, 16

  i) When the Bible refers to believers in Christ, it does not address them as **"dead"**, but as **"asleep"**. (Lazarus–John 11:11; comforting one another–1 Thessalonians 4:13-16; saints arose–Matthew 27:52)

d) All believers or supporters (using this loosely to illustrate a point) of Jesus will resurrect unto eternal life.

  i) If a person or team you are supporting goes to the ring and wins, you have also won. It is appropriate to celebrate that win and you aren't considered crazy for doing such. In the same way, Jesus our Champion won, so we all who have put our faith in Him (supporting Him), have won and are champions along with Him. We won with Him.

  ii) Jesus died on the cross and rose again, so all those who believe in Him will rise again because He did. We died with Him and we rose with Him.

H. Jesus is the Resurrection and the Life

  a) *"Jesus said unto her, I am the resurrection, and the life: he that believeth in me, though he were dead, yet shall he live: And whosoever liveth and believeth in me shall never die. Believest thou this?"* –John 11:25-26

  i) Though they were asleep, they will resurrect.

  b) *"I am the God of Abraham, and the God of Isaac, and the God of Jacob? God is not the God of the dead, but of the living."* –Matthew 22:32

Chapter Eleven

    i) God is the God of the living not the dead. He is the God of Resurrection.

I. Proof of forgiveness of our sins

Look no further, the resurrection of Jesus proves that we have been forgiven. Because of the resurrection of Jesus, we have proof and evidence that we have been forgiven of all our iniquities and our sins. Romans 4:25 says, *"who was delivered up because of our offenses, and was raised because of our justification."* (NJKV) Jesus was raised to secure and seal our justification (forgiveness). Because we are justified (acquitted), Jesus was raised from the dead.

    a) *"And you, being dead in your sins and the uncircumcision of your flesh, hath he quickened together with him, having forgiven you **all** trespasses;"* –Colossians 2:13 (emphasis mine)

    b) *"Who forgiveth all thine iniquities; who healeth all thy diseases;"* –Psalm 103:3 (emphasis mine)

    c) *"Neither by the blood of goats and calves, but by his own blood he entered in once into the holy place, having obtained eternal redemption for us. And for this cause he is the mediator of the new testament, that by means of death, for the redemption of the transgressions that were under the first testament, they which are called might receive the promise of eternal inheritance."* –Hebrews 9:12, 15

    d) *"By the which will we are sanctified through the offering of the body of Jesus Christ once for all. And every priest standeth daily ministering and offering oftentimes the same sacrifices, which can never take away sins: But this man, after he had offered one sacrifice for sins forever, sat down on the right hand of God;" For by one offering he hath perfected forever them that are sanctified."* –Hebrews 10:10-12, 14

        i) If Jesus did not resurrect from the dead, our sins cannot be forgiven. We have been completely forgiven of ALL our past, present and future sins have been forgiven. We have a new nature that does not want to sin.

ii) All our sins were in the future before we got saved and before we even sinned, yet Jesus died and paid for them. The payment and sacrifice of Jesus were a million times greater than our sin. Because of how vast the payment was (the blood of Jesus), how could we doubt that it could take care of all our sins—past, present, and future?

- If Jesus did not die and forgive our future sins, then we cannot be truly born again.
- It takes the sinless blood of Jesus for us to be forgiven (Hebrews 9:22), not an apology or I'm sorry. If all it took was to say sorry, then Jesus did not need to come. We could accomplish this another way. There was no way, so Jesus had to come.

iii) If Jesus did not pay for our past, present and future sins, then we are doomed. He won't be dying again. (Hebrews 9:27)

iv) Our redemption is not only good until the next time we sin. It is not partial but complete from the moment of salvation.

- The Old Testament forgiveness was temporal while the New Testament forgiveness was eternal. There is a big difference. Unlike the Old Testament priests who offered sacrifices daily or continually, Jesus did it once for all time and for all people. What a huge difference! This ONE TIME CLEANSED US FOR ALL TIME. (Hebrews 9:25-28).

3. The claims of Jesus about Himself

A close examination of the Scriptures reveals that Jesus knew who He was. Unlike other religions, Jesus claimed to be God. Many people were stunned by His claims, but they proved to be true as He continued to live His power-filled life. He was God incarnate. He never shied from it, and He openly declared it.

a) *"I and my father are one."*–John 10:30.

Chapter Eleven

b) *"I said therefore unto you, that ye shall die in your sins: for if ye believe not that I am he, ye shall die in your sins."*–John 8:24.

c) *"Which of you convinceth me of sin? And if I say the truth, why do ye not believe me?"*–John 8:46.

   i) Jesus never sinned.

d) *"Jesus saith unto him, I am the way, the truth, and the life: no man cometh unto the Father, but by me."*–John 14:6

   i) Jesus did not say He was **a** way, **a** truth, and **a** life.

   - He claimed to be the Way, the Truth and the Life.
   - This leaves no room for any other means of salvation.

   ii) This statement leaves no alternatives. Any religion that doesn't acknowledge Jesus as the ONLY way of salvation is in error and false.

   iii) Jesus is not just the way. He is also the truth and the life. If Jesus is not the LORD of your life, you have missed the truth. Jesus = Truth.

e) *"But if I do, though ye believe not me, believe the works: that ye may know, and believe, that the Father is in me, and I in him."* –John 10:38

   i) Miracles are great demonstrations of the power of God, and here Jesus tells the Jews to at least believe the miracles, signs, and wonders that He performed. Then they would know that He is God (one with the Father) and that Father is in Him, and He is in the Father. He was saying to consider the signs and wonders He performed. It would open their hearts to believe who He said He was. "I and the Father are one." (John 10:30)

f) *"That all men should honour the Son, even as they honour the Father. He that honoureth not the Son honoureth not the Father which hath sent him."*–John 5:23.

- i) Jesus claimed that ALL men should honor Him (the Son) the same way they honor the Father.

g) *"Then said they unto him, Where is thy Father? Jesus answered, Ye neither know me, nor my Father: if ye had known me, ye should have known my Father also."* –John 8:19

h) *"If ye had known me, ye should have known my Father also: and from henceforth ye know him, and have seen him."* –John 14:7

i) *"…he that receiveth me receiveth him that sent me."* –John 13:20

j) *"He that hateth me hateth my Father also."* –John 15:23

4. The burden of salvation

   a) All mankind knows that they have sinned and intuitively know that there will be a future eternal judgment for all sin by God. (Romans 1:18-22) Because of this intuitive knowledge, every religion is trying to do something to avert that coming judgment that awaits the life after this life.

      i) We live in a performance world. If you need to get paid, get promoted, have friends, have a good marriage, pretty much everything is based and directed by performance and good works.

      ii) You have to work for everything and that's good, but the kingdom of God works quite differently. We have transposed the way this world works for how the kingdom of God works.

   b) All religions have resorted to performance, good works and keeping the law as a means to earning right standing with God, which puts the heavy, unbearable burden and responsibility of salvation on the back of the individual.

      i) "You have to earn and work your way to heaven; you must be a good person," they claim.

Chapter Eleven

      ii) Question: How good do you have to be? God doesn't grade on a curve. (James 2:10) That's what all religions (Islam, Buddhism, Jehovah Witness, Jesuits, atheism, you name it) teach, but it is impossible to earn your way to heaven through good deeds and performance.

      iii) No man can truly carry that weight and expectation on their back. James 2:10 says, *"For whosoever shall keep the whole law, and yet offend in one point, he is guilty of all."*

c) Where Christianity differs from other religions among many other reasons, is that it doesn't put the responsibility and burden of salvation on the back of any person.

      i) That responsibility is on Jesus' back. He carried it for us (Isaiah 53:4-5) because He was God in the physical body. No one could do it. I don't care how good you think you are; you will fail. You will sin. You will come short. You can't do it perfectly like Jesus.

      ii) In Christianity, the burden of salvation is on the Lord Jesus Christ, the Savior of the world, not on any individual. We couldn't do it, and that's why Jesus did it for all of us. Quit trying! All it takes is to believe on the Lord Jesus and you will have His goodness deposited to your spiritual account only by putting faith in Him. Even if you were to be obedient, your obedience would fail in thought, word, and deed. The only standard of obedience that God accepts is the obedience of Jesus.

5. Every other religion teaches to earn our way and salvation to God

   a) *"But God commendeth his love toward us, in that, while we were yet sinners, Christ died for us."* –Romans 5:8

   b) Unlike all other religions, Christianity is not about performance and good deeds to earn, right standing, salvation, favor, and love of God. It teaches that no man can be good enough; therefore, all in need of a Savior.

c) We can't perform or work ourselves into the love of God, not even the blessing of God, or into heaven because we can't do it perfectly. If you cannot do it perfectly, you have failed.

   i) Even if you are better than me and your neighbor, you still come short of the standard of God.

   ii) God's standard is 100% if you make 99.99% you have failed, even though you are better than the guy with 70%.

   iii) It's one standard. God doesn't grade on a curve. You either make 100% or you have failed. If you are not perfect, you do not pass the test. (James 2:10)

   iv) No one can achieve perfection, and that's why Jesus (God) came to earth and became a man to pay for all our shortcomings.

   v) He did it to fulfill the law for us, because we couldn't. He then deposited His grade and marks to our individual spiritual account through ONLY believing and putting faith in Him. It's so simple and takes the pressure off of you.

   vi) It entirely removes the burden of performing to save ourselves and earning relationship with God off your back.

d) Since only believing in Jesus is the way into relationship, salvation and right standing with God, every person has a fair shot; good or bad, better or worse, 99.99% or 85%, if they only believe in Jesus that He died for their sin and rose again from the dead.

6. Not a list of do's and don'ts

   a) Christianity is not a list of do's and don'ts to enter a relationship with God like many religions teach.

   b) Believing in Jesus is the great equalizer among people. Bad and good, we can all choose to believe, regardless of our good or bad works and performance!

- c) The only way to receive salvation is by faith, not by works and good performance.

    - i) Acts 16:31–Faith in Jesus and the finished work of the cross, not our works is the only requirement for salvation. (John 6:28-29; Acts 15:9; 16:30-33; Mark 16:16; John 1:12, 3:15-16, 36, 20:3; Romans 5:1-2, 10:9-10; Galatians 3:22, 26; Ephesians 2:8-9; Romans 3:20-31)

    - ii) Faith in Jesus and what Jesus did for us is the only requirement for salvation and the only thing we can do to receive salvation.

- d) Although our actions are important, they do not produce salvation, right standing with God, or relationship with God.

    - i) Our performances or actions are not the root to our salvation and right standing with God, but just the fruit of that relationship.

    - ii) All religions teach the opposite of this.

- e) We cannot work or perform our way into heaven.

- f) We can only believe our way into it. Christianity is a relationship with God through Jesus, not a set of rules to earn us right standing with God.

7. The Bible

    - a) The Bible is the Word of God, which is the basis of the Christian faith. According to the Bible, Jesus and the Word are one. *"In the beginning was the Word, and the Word was with God, and the Word was God."*–John 1:1

    - b) The Bible is infallible, incorruptible, and inspired by God (2 Timothy 3:16) and it is the truth. (John 17:17)

8. Hope for a no-judgment eternity and life after death

    - a) *"If in this life only we have hope in Christ, we are of all men most miserable."*–1 Corinthians 15:19

i) No religion offers real hope of life after death except for Christianity. Every person alive has asked the questions, "where do I go after I die?" and "what is it like after this life?", but only Christianity has a satisfying answer. This mystery strikes fear in almost anyone alive, even the so-called atheists.

ii) There is no atheist on a deathbed. Suddenly, they are forced to begin to think and consider life after death. Sadly enough, they have no answer. Some just dismiss it and others just come up with whatever makes them feel good.

iii) For other religions, there is no certainty of what will happen on the other side after this life. They all hope they make it to safety and paradise.

iv) Christianity is certain about life after death.

- Those who believe in the Champion of resurrection, Jesus, will also resurrect to spend eternity with Him.

b) *"Jesus said unto her, I am the resurrection, and the life: he that believeth in me, though he were dead, yet shall he live:"*–John 11:25.

Because Jesus resurrected, Christianity teaches that the believers in Jesus will also resurrect from the dead and live life eternal with Jesus. There will not be eternal damnation for Christians, and it is a settled truth that brings hope like no other religion.

i) *"We are **confident**, I say, and willing rather to be absent from the body, and to be present with the Lord."* –2 Corinthians 5:8 (emphasis mine)

- A Christian is confident of the life after death.
- The Champion of Christians, Jesus Christ, defeated death and the grave, and those who put faith in Him will experience the same.

Chapter Eleven

- ii) "For to me to live is Christ, and to die is gain."–Philippians 1:21

    ○ A Christian sees death as gain because of the certain assurance and hope to be with Jesus in the next life and not experience judgment.

- iii) *"For I am in a strait betwixt two, having a desire to depart, and to be with Christ; which is far better:"*–Philippians 1:23

    ○ Paul reveals that to be with the Lord is far better. He was speaking about death. For a believer being with the Lord is far better than the best thing this world could offer.

9. The sinlessness of Jesus

    The sinlessness of Jesus is a vital Christian doctrine. It is foundational to Christianity because if Jesus had been a sinner Himself, then He too would have needed a Savior. But Jesus was so pure that even His enemies attested to His innocence and purity.

    a) *"Which of you convinceth me of sin? And if I say the truth, why do ye not believe me?"* –John 8:46

    b) *"Who did no sin, neither was guile found in his mouth."* –1 Peter 2:22

    c) *"And he made his grave with the wicked, and with the rich in his death; because he had done no violence, neither was any deceit in his mouth."* – Isaiah 53:9

    d) *"For we have not a high priest which cannot be touched with the feeling of our infirmities; but was in all points tempted like as were, yet without sin."* –Hebrews 4:15

        i) This verse clearly states that although Jesus became like one of us and was tempted (Matt. 4:1-4) like all of us, He was still without sin.

e) *"For such an high priest became us, who is holy, harmless, undefiled, separate from sinners, and made higher than the heavens;"* –Hebrews 7:26

I pray that some of the evidence I have laid out helps you solidify your relationship with Him, but if you do not know Him, come into relationship with the Lord. If you do not know Jesus, you are missing out on both in this life and the one to come.

Chapter Twelve

What is the Fear of the Lord?

The fear of the Lord is one of the most mentioned subjects in the Word of God, yet it is not spoken about as much. One question we all must answer regularly is, Do I have the fear of God and am I walking in it?

What is the fear of God?

Before I define the fear of the Lord, I must say that we have the grace (God's enabling power and ability that is undeserved, unearned, and unmerited) to walk in the fear of the Lord. For everything the Lord asks us to do, He equips and empowers us to do it. We should not do anything in our own strength. God works in us both to will and to do for His good pleasure. (Philippians 2:13)

The fear of God is simply an awe; reverence, respect, and honor of God. The fear of the Lord is above all **worshiping the Lord**. As you read along, you will see that there are more facets to the fear of the Lord which I explain further down in the chapter.

Jesus was quoting Deuteronomy 6:13 in Matthew 4:10, but the choice of His words is telling us about the fear of God.

a) *"Thou shalt fear the Lord thy God, and serve him, and shalt swear by his name."* –Deuteronomy 6:13

b) *"Then saith Jesus unto him, Get thee hence, Satan: for it is written, thou shalt worship the Lord thy God, and him only shalt thou serve."* –Matthew 4:10

   i) Jesus used *"Worship the Lord thy God"* in Matthew 4:10 interchangeably with *"Fear the Lord thy God"* as quoted in Deuteronomy 6:13.

   ii) Therefore to fear the Lord is to worship the Lord. Those who have rejected the Lord do not have the fear of the Lord because they are worshiping something else other than Him who is the Lord God. Those who aren't born again do not have the fear of the Lord. Jesus was and is God (1 Timothy 3:16) and ought to be worshipped. Those who do truly have the fear of the Lord.

   - Fear of the Lord = Worshipping Jesus = Worshipping the Lord thy God

These verses show Jesus rightfully being worshipped:
Matthew 2:11–wise men from the east
Matthew 8:2–a leper
Matthew 9:18–Jairus
Matthew 14:33–Jesus walks on water and goes to the boat
Matthew 15:25–Canaanite woman
Matthew 20:20–Mother of Zebedee's children (James and John)
Matthew 28:9–Mary Magdalene and the other Mary
Matthew 28:17–some of the disciples after His resurrection
Mark 5:6–a man with an unclean spirit that was dwelling in the tombs
Luke 24:52–the disciples at His ascending
John 9:38–the lame man that was healed in John

The command to fear the Lord

We need to make a commitment to the Lord to walk in the fear of Him, and He will help us uphold that commitment. This is a big deal and the missing ingredient in the life of many believers and yet it is the most important. If we

Chapter Twelve

are doing our own thing, we aren't walking in the fear of the Lord. We need to commit before we fit.

The Word of God commands us to fear the Lord. These verses below reveal that this is not a choice, nor is it something to be done by just a few zealots or preachers.

a) *"Now these [are] the commandments, the statutes, and the judgments, which the LORD your God commanded to teach you, that ye might do [them] in the land whither ye go to possess it: That thou mightest fear the LORD thy God, to keep all his statutes and his commandments, which I command thee, thou, and thy son, and thy son's son, all the days of thy life; and that thy days may be prolonged."* –Deuteronomy 6:1-2

b) *"Thou shalt fear the LORD thy God, and serve him, and shalt swear by his name."* –Deuteronomy 6:13

c) *"And the LORD commanded us to do all these statutes, to fear the LORD our God, for our good always, that he might preserve us alive, as [it is] at this day."* –Deuteronomy 6:24

d) *"Therefore thou shalt keep the commandments of the LORD thy God, to walk in his ways, and to fear him."* –Deuteronomy 8:6

e) *"And now, Israel, what doth the LORD thy God require of thee, but to fear the LORD thy God, to walk in all his ways, and to love him, and to serve the LORD thy God with all thy heart and with all thy soul, To keep the commandments of the LORD, and his statutes, which I command thee this day for thy good?"* –Deuteronomy 10:12-13

f) *"Thou shalt fear the LORD thy God; him shalt thou serve, and to him shalt thou cleave, and swear by his name."* –Deuteronomy 10:20

g) *"Ye shall walk after the LORD your God, and fear him, and keep his commandments, and obey his voice, and ye shall serve him, and cleave unto him."* –Deuteronomy 13:4

h) *"Now therefore fear the LORD, and serve him in sincerity and in truth: and put away the gods which your fathers served on the other side of the flood, and in Egypt; and serve ye the LORD."* –Joshua 24:14

1. The fear of the Lord has to be taught and learned

    Did you know that the fear of the Lord has to be taught? If it has to be taught, this means it does not come naturally. No one is born with the fear of the Lord, that is why we have to be born again. Why were the people in the Old Testament told to fear the Lord when they were not born again? I believe it was to drive them to dependency upon God to achieve the desired result. A heart change is required to effectively walk in the fear of the Lord; otherwise, it will be sporadic. If I told an unbeliever to fear God, I would be showing them the impossibility of that so that they can give up and ask for help and be born again.

    You do not just wake up with the fear of the Lord. It is going to take some effort on our part and some renewing of the mind. (Romans 12:1-2)

    a) *"Thou shalt truly tithe all the increase of thy seed, that the field bringeth forth year by year. And thou shalt eat before the LORD thy God, in the place which he shall choose to place his name there, the tithe of thy corn, of thy wine, and of thine oil, and the firstlings of thy herds and of thy flocks; that thou mayest **learn to fear the LORD thy God always**."* –Deuteronomy 14:22-23 (emphasis mine).

        i) Notice that the fear of the Lord has to be learned. It does not happen automatically or naturally. This passage reveals that the way the Israelites were to demonstrate their fear of the Lord was in the giving of their tithes to Him.

    b) *"Then one of the priests whom they had carried away from Samaria came and dwelt in Beth-el, and **taught them how they should fear the LORD**."* –2 Kings 17:28 (emphasis mine).

    c) *"Come, ye children, hearken unto me: I will teach you the fear of the LORD."* –Psalm 34:11

Chapter Twelve

      i) This learning comes through the Word of God (Deuteronomy 17:18-20). As we read the Word, we learn to fear God.

d) *"Then Zerubbabel the son of Shealtiel, and Joshua the son of Josedech, the high priest, with all the remnant of the people, obeyed the voice of the LORD their God, and the words of Haggai the prophet, as the LORD their God had sent him, and the people did fear before the LORD."* –Haggai 1:12

e) *"Only take heed to thyself, and keep thy soul diligently, lest thou forget the things which thine eyes have seen, and lest they depart from thy heart all the days of thy life: but teach them thy sons, and thy sons' sons; [Specially] the day that thou stoodest before the LORD thy God in Horeb, when the LORD said unto me, Gather me the people together, and* **I will make them hear my words, that they may learn to fear me all the days that they shall live upon the earth, and [that] they may teach their children."** –Deuteronomy 4:9-10 (emphasis mine)

      i) Notice that when we hear His words (voice), we will learn to fear Him.

f) *"And thou shalt stone him with stones, that he die; because he hath sought to thrust thee away from the LORD thy God, which brought thee out of the land of Egypt, from the house of bondage. And all Israel shall hear, and fear, and shall do no more any such wickedness as this is among you.* (Deuteronomy 17:12-13; 19:16-20). –Deuteronomy 13:10-11.

      i) This passage reveals that if we want people to fear the Lord, we need to deal with certain behaviors that they manifest contrary to God's Word, so they hear and fear. This is why in many cases we see the death penalty or other actions from authorities such as jail or prison. If no action is ever taken against sin, people will not learn the fear of God. Rather than just using punishment upon the evildoer, the fear of the Lord ought to be taught. (Psalm 34:11)

2. Be in the fear of the Lord all day long

    a) *"Let not thine heart envy sinners: but be thou in the fear of the LORD all the day long."* –Proverbs 23:17

        i) We ought to be in the fear of the Lord not only for a part of the day.

3. All the inhabitants of the world

    a) *"Let all the earth fear the LORD: let all the inhabitants of the world stand in awe of him."* –Psalm 33:8

        i) The fear of the Lord is not just for the clergy or the preachers, but the entire world. We have no excuse not to fear the Lord.

4. A person who says there is no God is not only a fool, but has no fear, reverence, and honor of the Lord.

    a) *"The fool hath said in his heart, [There is] no God. They are corrupt, they have done abominable works, [there is] none that doeth good."* –Psalm 14:1

    b) *"The fool hath said in his heart, [There is] no God. Corrupt are they, and have done abominable iniquity: [there is] none that doeth good."* –Psalm 53:1

Examples of fearing the Lord:

1. Jesus

    a) *"And there shall come forth a rod out of the stem of Jesse, and a Branch shall grow out of his roots: And the spirit of the LORD shall rest upon him, the spirit of wisdom and understanding, the spirit of counsel and might, the spirit of knowledge and of the <u>fear of the LORD</u>; And shall make him of quick understanding in <u>the fear of the LORD</u>: and he shall not judge after the sight of his eyes, neither reprove after the hearing of his ears:* –Isaiah 11:1-3 (Parentheses mine).

       i) This prophecy is about the Lord Jesus. Jesus had, and walked in, the fear of God.

       ii) He was and is the best example of the fear of the Lord.

2. Joseph

   a) *"There is none greater in this house than I; neither hath he kept back any thing from me but thee, because thou art his wife: how then can I do this great wickedness, and sin against God?"* –Genesis 39:9

       i) Joseph revealed to us why he would not have sexual relations with Potiphar's wife. It is because he had a fear of the Lord. He did not want to sin against God. He saw this sin as a sin against God, not Potiphar, although it would have been a sin against him. He had a greater and bigger cause why he would not commit sin. He feared God. He worshipped, honored, and reverenced God more than man.

3. Early church

   a) *"Then had the churches rest throughout all Judaea and Galilee and Samaria, and were edified; and walking in the fear of the Lord, and in the comfort of the Holy Ghost, were multiplied."* –Acts 9:31

   b) *"Submitting yourselves one to another in the fear of God."* –Ephesians 5:21

   c) *"Nevertheless let every one of you in particular so love his wife even as himself; and the wife [see] that she reverence [her] husband."* –Ephesians 5:33

       i) The same word that was translated fear in Ephesians 5:21 was translated reverence here in Ephesians 5:33. Of course this is not talking about a fear that is only reserved for the Lord such as worship. This passages reveals that one of the ways a wife can fear the Lord is to reverence her husband. Not reverencing her husband is not fearing God.

d) *"But sanctify the Lord God in your hearts: and [be] ready always to [give] an answer to every man that asketh you a reason of the hope that is in you with meekness and fear:"* –1 Peter 3:15

4. Daniel and three friends feared God more than the king

    Daniel feared God and would not compromise. One of the reasons we compromise is because we do not have the fear of the Lord. The fear of the Lord will keep us from compromise.

    a) *"But Daniel purposed in his heart that he would not defile himself with the portion of the king's meat, nor with the wine which he drank: therefore he requested of the prince of the eunuchs that he might not defile himself."* – Daniel 1:8

    b) *"Shadrach, Meshach, and Abednego, answered and said to the king, O Nebuchadnezzar, we are not careful to answer thee (not afraid) in this matter. If it be so, our God whom we serve is able to deliver us from the burning fiery furnace, and he will deliver us out of thine hand, O king. But if not, be it known unto thee, O king, that we will not serve thy gods, nor worship the golden image which thou hast set up."* –Daniel 3:16-18

    c) *"Now when Daniel knew that the writing was signed, he went into his house; and his windows being open in his chamber toward Jerusalem, he kneeled upon his knees three times a day, and prayed, and gave thanks before his God, as he did aforetime."* –Daniel 6:10

5. Job

    a) *"There was a man in the land of Uz, whose name was Job; and that man was perfect and upright, and one that feared God, and eschewed evil."* –Job 1:1

        i) This text says that Job eschewed evil, which means he abstained from and shunned evil. We won't truly abstain from something we do not hate, because when we hate something, we lose the desire to participate in it. Shunning and abstaining from evil leads to a departure from it.

ii) Notice that there is no genuine fear of the Lord that excludes hatred for evil. (Proverbs 3:5-9; 14:16) One of the major deterrents of sin is to develop a hatred for it. Very few people will do what they hate. We cannot separate hatred for evil from fearing God.

More on what the fear of the Lord is

1. Beginning of wisdom

    a) *"The fear of the LORD [is] the beginning of wisdom: a good understanding have all they that do [his commandments]: his praise endureth for ever."* – Psalm 111:10

    b) *"The fear of the LORD [is] the beginning of wisdom: and the knowledge of the holy [is] understanding."* –Proverbs 9:10

    c) *"The fear of the LORD [is] the instruction of wisdom; and before honour [is] humility."* –Proverbs 15:33

2. Beginning of knowledge

    a) *"The fear of the LORD [is] the beginning of knowledge: [but] fools despise wisdom and instruction."* –Proverbs 1:7

        i) Knowledge precedes wisdom, but both begin with the fear of Lord.

3. Loving the Lord

    a) *"And shewing mercy unto thousands of them that love me, and keep my commandments"* –Exodus 20:6

    b) *"And his mercy [is] on them that fear him from generation to generation."* –Luke 1:50

        i) These two verses use the words *"fear Him"* and *"love me"* interchangeably.

        ii) To fear the Lord is to love the Lord, and to love the Lord is to fear the Lord.

b) *"**Ye that love the LORD, hate evil**: he preserveth the souls of his saints; he delivereth them out of the hand of the wicked."* –Psalm 97:10

   i) If we love the Lord, we need to hate evil, which is also the fear of the Lord (Proverbs 8:13). Again, loving the Lord does not go without hating evil. Those who love the Lord will hate evil.

   ii) Loving the Lord = fearing God = hating evil.

4. Loving the good

   a) *"Hate the evil, and love the good, and establish judgment in the gate: it may be that the LORD God of hosts will be gracious unto the remnant of Joseph."* –Amos 5:15

      i) Hating evil is the fearing of the Lord. When we hate evil, it is because we love what is good. Again, it is impossible to love good and not hate evil. Those who claim to love what is good, but do not have a hatred for evil are deceived and they do not have the fear of the Lord.

         ○ Hating evil = fearing God = loving the good

      ii) Many people do not have a fear of the Lord because of their love for the things of this world. We cannot love the world and love God at the same time. It's impossible. We need to choose one and give up on the other.

         ○ *"Love not the world, neither the things that are in the world. If any man love the world, the love of the Father is not in him. For all that is in the world, the lust of the flesh, and the lust of the eyes, and the pride of life, is not of the Father, but is of the world."* –1 John 2:15-16

         ○ "World" is defined by verse 16 as "the lust of the flesh, and the lust of the eyes, and the pride of life." This is not saying we hate people rather we love not the things in the world which are defined by the things above–the lust of the flesh, and the lust of the eyes, and the pride of life

5. Fearing the Lord is trusting the Lord

   a) "**Ye that fear the LORD, trust in the LORD:** he [is] their help and their shield. The LORD hath been mindful of us: he will bless [us]; he will bless the house of Israel; he will bless the house of Aaron. He will bless them that fear the LORD, [both] small and great." –Psalm 115:11-13 (emphasis mine)

      i) If you are trusting in yourself and your own goodness, you do not fear God. Fearing God is trusting God. If we aren't trusting God, we aren't fearing Him.

   b) "The fear of man bringeth a snare: but whoso putteth his trust in the LORD shall be safe." –Proverbs 29:25

      i) The opposite of fearing man is fearing God.

      ii) Someone has defined the fear of the Lord as fearing nothing else. To fear God is to fear nothing else, not man, death, sickness or disease. Why? Because He tells us to fear not. Fearing is going contrary to what He instructs us and it's not fearing Him.

      iii) The fear of the Lord is not terror. Jesus has borne our judgment. (John 12:32)

   c) "And he hath put a new song in my mouth, [even] praise unto our God: many shall see [it], and fear, and shall trust in the LORD." –Psalm 40:3

6. Fear of the Lord is departing from evil

   a) "Trust in the LORD with all thine heart; and lean not unto thine own understanding. In all thy ways acknowledge him, and he shall direct thy paths. Be not wise in thine own eyes: **fear the LORD, and depart from evil.** It shall be health to thy navel, and marrow to thy bones. Honour the

GOT QUESTIONS?

LORD with thy substance, and with the firstfruits of all thine increase:" – Proverbs 3:5-9 (emphasis mine)

  i) Those who truly love the Lord will depart from evil. Claiming to love the Lord and not departing from evil is not the fear of the Lord. A genuine fear and reverence of the Lord will cause a person to depart from evil.

  ii) Trusting the Lord, acknowledging Him in all our ways, and not being wise in our own eyes are all characteristics of fearing the Lord.

b) *"A wise man feareth, and departeth from evil: but the fool rageth, and is confident."*–Proverbs 14:16

  i) This is talking about a reverential kind of fear. A fear that is toward the Lord, not people or terror. Fearing the Lord causes a departure from evil. To fear the Lord is to depart from evil.

c) *"By mercy and truth iniquity is purged: and by the fear of the LORD [men] depart from evil."* –Proverbs 16:6

  i) One of the reasons people sin is because they have no fear of the Lord. The more we fear the Lord, the more godly we will become.

d) *"The highway of the upright is to depart from evil: he that keepeth his way preserveth his soul."* –Proverbs 16:17

  i) A highway is a main road. In the same way, the main road for the upright is departing from evil. Highways help us travel faster, safer and without obstacles. This is what the fear of the Lord does for us. The fear of the Lord will cause us to go far and achieve the call of God in our lives.

  ii) The fear of the Lord can also be likened to a staircase by which we can climb higher.

Chapter Twelve

7. Fearing the Lord is not just to depart from evil, but to hate evil.

    Fearing the Lord = hating evil.

    a) *"Ye that love the LORD, hate evil: he preserveth the souls of his saints; he delivereth them out of the hand of the wicked."* –Psalm 97:10

    b) *"The fear of the LORD [is] to hate evil: pride, and arrogancy, and the evil way, and the froward mouth, do I hate."* –Proverbs 8:13 (emphasis mine)

        i) Fearing the Lord is to hate evil. Those who don't hate evil don't fear God. It is all talk and no action.

        ii) According to this verse, the true fear of the Lord is to hate evil. God hates pride, arrogance, the evil way, and the froward mouth. Notice that He doesn't hate people who do these things, but He hates these acts. There is a huge difference. We need to hate what the Lord hates.

    c) *"Let love be without dissimulation. Abhor that which is evil; cleave to that which is good."* –Romans 12:9

        i) Genuine love is without hypocrisy. It has a hatred for evil. When we hate evil, we cleave to what is good.

        ii) We won't depart from what we do not hate. We need to work on our capacity to hate–no, not people but evil. If you do not hate evil, sin, and ungodliness, you will participate in it.

    d) *"Be ye angry, and sin not: let not the sun go down upon your wrath: Neither give place to the devil."* –Ephesians 4:26-27

        i) *"Submit yourselves therefore to God. Resist the devil, and he will flee from you."* –James 4:7

        ii) One of the ways to hate evil is by being angry at sin, hence, resisting the devil.

- Those who have no hatred for evil will not resist the devil.

iii) Jesus was angry at sin and made a whip and drove merchants out of the temple. He did this twice (at the beginning and at the end).

- John 2:14-17; Matthew 21:12-16; Mark 11:15-18; Luke 19:45-46.

iv) **"Stand in awe, and sin not:** commune with your own heart upon your bed, and be still. Selah." –Psalm 4:4 (emphasis mine)

- The word "awe" here means to be angry (see the NKJV, and the Amplified). This is talking about a godly anger as in Ephesians 4:26-27.
- If we aren't angry, we will sin. Anger is meant to fight against sin and evil and its author, Satan.

8. Giving our tithes and/or offerings

a) "Be not wise in thine own eyes: fear the LORD, and depart from evil. 8 It shall be health to thy navel, and marrow to thy bones. **Honour the LORD with thy substance**, and with the firstfruits of all thine increase: So shall thy barns be filled with plenty, and thy presses shall burst out with new wine." –Proverbs 3:7-10 (emphasis mine)

   i) Those who do not fear the Lord are not givers. Giving honors the Lord. If we do not give, we are not honoring the Lord and aren't walking in the fear of the Lord. You may think, but wait a minute. So and so and I have nothing to give. Not true! God would never ask anyone to give if they had nothing. I do not believe there is anyone on earth that has nothing to give to the Lord. It may not be literal money, but people can give if they want to. The issue is wrong priorities among others.

b) "Thou shalt truly tithe all the increase of thy seed, that the field bringeth forth year by year. And thou shalt eat before the LORD thy God, in the place which he shall choose to place his name there, the tithe of thy corn, of

Chapter Twelve

thy wine, and of thine oil, and the firstlings of thy herds and of thy flocks; that thou mayest learn to fear the LORD thy God always." –Deuteronomy 14:22-23

    i) This passage reveals that the fear of the Lord is being faithful in giving our tithes. This has to be taught just as the fear of the Lord must be taught. When we learn to fear the Lord, we faithfully give.

9. Walking in uprightness

   a) "He that walketh in his uprightness feareth the LORD: but he that is perverse in his ways despiseth him." –Proverbs 14:2

      i) Walking in uprightness is fearing the Lord. Those who aren't walking in a godly manner do not fear the Lord.

      ii) This is talking about someone who is living right and godly; one who is walking in a righteous lifestyle.

10. Walking in integrity

   a) "The just man walketh in his integrity: his children are blessed after him." –Proverbs 20:7

      i) Walking in integrity is profitable not only to us, but also to those who surround and associate with us. Our children can and will reap blessings from our integrity and uprightness. The opposite is true as well. Those who walk in dishonesty and a lack of character not only affect their lives, but the lives of their children and those associated with them.

11. Not taking advantage of others

   a) "Thou shalt not curse the deaf, nor put a stumblingblock before the blind, but shalt fear thy God: I [am] the LORD." –Leviticus 19:14

      i) Mistreating the deaf, cursing them, being profane toward them because they can't hear us is not fearing the Lord.

- The deaf can be extended to mean taking advantage of those who have not heard or have missed a vital communication about something.
        ii) Setting traps and taking advantage of the blind because they can't see is not fearing the Lord. This includes lying and cheating those who may not be knowledgeable about something.

12. Not oppressing one another

    a) "Ye shall not therefore oppress one another; but thou shalt fear thy God: for I [am] the LORD your God." –Leviticus 25:17

13. Fear of those in Authority

    a) "My son, fear thou the LORD and the king: and meddle not with them that are given to change:"–Proverbs 24:21

        i) Fear of the Lord is honoring those in authority. Of course, this does not include compliance with ungodly commands. Refusing to respect, honor, and obey the king, or authority, is not walking in the fear of the Lord.

        ii) We are to fear not just the Lord, but the king (those in authority) and not mingle or intermix with those who are given to rebellion.

        iii) "Let every soul be subject unto the higher powers. For there is no power but of God: the powers that be are ordained of God. ²Whosoever therefore resisteth the power, resisteth the ordinance of God: and they that resist shall receive to themselves damnation. ³For rulers are not a terror to good works, but to the evil. Wilt thou then not be afraid of the power? do that which is good, and thou shalt have praise of the same: ⁴For he is the minister of God to thee for good. But if thou do that which is evil, be afraid; for he beareth not the sword in vain: for he is the minister of God, a revenger to execute wrath upon him that doeth evil. ⁵Wherefore ye must needs be subject, not only for wrath, but also for conscience sake." –Romans 13:1-5

Chapter Twelve

Advantages or benefits of fearing God

1. Fear of the Lord produces holiness

    a) *"Having therefore these promises, dearly beloved, let us cleanse ourselves from all filthiness of the flesh and spirit, perfecting holiness in the fear of God."* –2 Corinthians 7:1

        i) Holiness is perfected in the fear of God. We can't live holy if we do not have the fear of God.

2. Fearing God is always for our good

    a) *"And the LORD commanded us to do all these statutes, to fear the LORD our God, for our good always, that he might preserve us alive, as [it is] at this day."* –Deuteronomy 6:24

    b) *"O that there were such an heart in them, that they would fear me, and keep all my commandments always, that it might be well with them, and with their children forever!"* –Deuteronomy 5:29

        i) Fearing the Lord is always for our own good and wellness. Those who refuse to fear the Lord will miss out on having things go well for them.

3. Releases the blessing of God in our lives

    a) *"Ye that fear the LORD, trust in the LORD: he is their help and their shield. The LORD hath been mindful of us: he will bless us; he will bless the house of Israel; he will bless the house of Aaron.* **He will bless them that fear the LORD, both small and great.***"* –Psalm 115:11-13 (emphasis mine)

4. No want/lack

    a) *"O fear the LORD, ye his saints: for there is no want to them that fear him."* –Psalm 34:9

5. It pleases the Lord

    a) *"The LORD taketh pleasure in them that fear him, in those that hope in his mercy."* –Psalm 147:11

        i) The Lord is delighted in us fearing Him. It brings Him joy and pleasure.

6. The fear of the Lord prolongs days

    a) *"The fear of the LORD prolongeth days: but the years of the wicked shall be shortened."* –Proverbs 10:27

    b) *"The fear of the LORD is a fountain of life, to depart from the snares of death."* – Proverbs 14:27

    c) *"The fear of the LORD [tendeth] to life: and [he that hath it] shall abide satisfied; he shall not be visited with evil."* –Proverbs 19:23

        i) These verses reveal that a lack of a fear for the Lord will shorten our days. We need to purpose to be in the fear of the Lord.

7. Satisfaction

    a) *"The fear of the LORD [tendeth] to life: and [he that hath it] shall abide satisfied; he shall not be visited with evil."* –Proverbs 19:23

        i) The fear of the Lord causes us to remain, abide, live in satisfaction and have need for nothing. If we are not abiding satisfied, we need to look at our fear of the Lord because he that has it shall abide satisfied.

        ii) Because we have the fear of the Lord, we are satisfied and won't go out and do certain ungodly things.

8. Not visited by evil

    a) *"The fear of the LORD [tendeth] to life: and [he that hath it] shall abide satisfied; he shall not be visited with evil."* –Proverbs 19:23

Chapter Twelve

> i) This is not to say that evil will never come against us (2 Timothy 3:12), but when we are in the fear of the Lord, we can stop the visitation of many evils. The fear of the Lord protects us from self-inflicted wounds. We live in a fallen world and evil will come, but not from the Lord. We have an assurance of safety and protection from it. The fear of the Lord will bring satisfaction and, in the end, will protect us from making decisions that could bring evil upon us.
>
> ii) We may be afflicted, but we have a promise of deliverance from all.
>
> - *"Many are the afflictions of the righteous: but the LORD delivereth him out of them all."* –Psalm 34:19

9. The fear of the Lord gives us confidence

   a) *"In the fear of the LORD [is] strong confidence: and his children shall have a place of refuge."* –Proverbs 14:26

   > i) If we want to have confidence, we need to walk in the fear of the Lord. This is one crucial way to get strong confidence. If we are lacking in strong confidence, we know the cause–a lack of the fear of the Lord.

10. Riches, honor and life

    a) *"By humility [and] the fear of the LORD [are] riches, and honour, and life."* –Proverbs 22:4

    > i) The fear of the Lord brings godly riches, honor, and life. If we want these things, we have to start from the fear of the Lord.

    b) *"Better [is] little with the fear of the LORD than great treasure and trouble therewith."* –Proverbs 15:16

    > i) Most people want more this and more that but the Word of God makes it clear that having more has no benefit if it is not done right, godly–in the fear of the Lord.

- Little is not less or insgnifcant if it has the fear of the Lord and is done in godliness. This is the very opposite of the get-more culture we live in. Many People will do anything ungodly to increase and get what they want.

11. Fear of the Lord is a treasure

    a) "And wisdom and knowledge shall be the stability of thy times, [and] strength of salvation: the fear of the LORD [is] his treasure." –Isaiah 33:6

        i) Many people are busy seeking treasures and so forth, but this passage reveals that fearing the Lord is a treasure—His treasure. What a deal!

        ii) The fear of the Lord ought to be the most sought after than anything else.

12. Antidote to envy

    a) "Let not thine heart envy sinners: but be thou in the fear of the LORD all the day long." –Proverbs 23:17

        i) We need to be in the fear of the Lord all day long (all the time), not just a part of the day or just at certain times. This is speaking of a continuity in fearing the Lord. If we do, one of the benefits is that our hearts will be guarded from envy.

            - "For where envying and strife is, there is confusion and every evil work." –James 3:16

        ii) One of the ways we can accomplish that is by keeping our minds stayed upon the Lord.

13. Happiness

    a) "Happy is the man that feareth alway: but he that hardeneth his heart shall fall into mischief." –Proverbs 28:14

Chapter Twelve

i) This is speaking about reverence and the fear of God. Those who fear God are happy. What does this say about those who do not fear the Lord? Their hearts are hardened and they are not happy. Our happiness is directly proportional to our fear of the Lord. To the degree that we fear the Lord is to the degree that we experience happiness. Those who are looking for happiness while excluding the fear of the Lord have missed the blessing that comes with it which is happiness.

ii) Note that this passage says ALWAYS. We need to fear the Lord always, not sporadically. Many fear the Lord, but they do that occasionally. We need to be consistent in the fear of the Lord.

iii) We also learn that those who are heart hardened, have no fear of the Lord and therefore fall into mischief.

In conclusion,

"Let us hear the conclusion of the whole matter: Fear God, and keep his commandments: for this [is] the whole [duty] of man."

–Ecclesiastes 12:13

Chapter Thirteen

Does God use or send problems to teach and perfect Us?

There are many teachings out there about how God teaches His children. Many say that God uses hardships, tragedies, sicknesses, and heartbreaks to teach, perfect, and disciple us. This is inaccurate. Before I discuss how God teaches us, I want to take time and discuss how He does not teach us.

a) If God used problems to teach us, then all of us should be perfected by now. If it's the problems that perfect us, then what does the Word of God do? If you look around and within, it is true that the most troubled, most diseased, and those with the most hardships and problems aren't the most mature and perfected believers.

b) It would be inconsistent for Jesus to go about healing all that were sick and oppressed of the devil (Acts 10:38) if it is tragedies, and problems that perfected them. No one can name one person who Jesus put sickness on or any form of problem to teach, mature, or perfect them. Jesus did the will of the Father to perfection (John 4:34). He was the full manifestation of God and He embodied His fullness (Colossians 1:15,19; Hebrews 1:3). By seeing Jesus, we have seen the Father (John 14:9).

   i) If you had a daughter and you wanted to teach her that sex outside marriage is wrong, you would not expose her to ungodly situations so you can teach her? That would not be an appropriate way to teach her.

ii) We can learn either through the Word or by the school of hard knocks. Yes, we still can learn through bad things that happen to us, but that is not God's way of teaching, growing or perfecting us.

iii) We can learn God's way (through the Word) or we can learn life's way (the school of hard knocks). We can learn either way, but not all ways are created equal. One is better than the other. One is God's preferred choice than the other.

"Thine own wickedness shall correct thee, and thy backslidings shall reprove thee: know therefore and see that it is an evil thing and bitter, that thou hast forsaken the LORD thy God, and that my fear is not in thee, saith the Lord GOD of hosts."

–Jeremiah 2:19

"Thy way and thy doings have procured these things unto thee; this is thy wickedness, because it is bitter, because it reacheth unto thine heart."

–Jeremiah 4:18.

These verses demonstrate that we can learn through the school of hard knocks. We can learn as a result of our wrongdoings, our sin, and our mistakes (if we choose to learn). We can be reproved and corrected through these means, but these means are not God's way of correcting us.

A lack of relationship, study and depth of the Word of God in some people's lives is why some people blame God for their problems and conclude that He teaches them through all these hardships and difficulties. No parent, especially a godly one, wishes harm or evil upon their children so they can learn. How would you like to teach your child? Would you put disease or kill your child in order for them to grow and mature?

If God were the one who put some sort of sickness on me to teach me, I would have nothing to do with that God, and neither should you. I am here to tell you that it is not God who puts sickness or tragedy on you to teach you.

Chapter Thirteen

- i) Thinking that God is the one who does that evil defies common sense, let alone the Word of God, and unfortunately, many fall for it.

- ii) If God uses all these miserable tragedies to teach us, then He is not a good God. The truth is there is nothing good about cancer, birth defects, failure, loss, death, or divorce.

- iii) John 10:10 makes it clear who is responsible for all the bad stuff. It says, *"The thief cometh not, but for to steal, and to kill, and to destroy: I am come that they might have life, and that they might have it more abundantly."*

a) *"In everything give thanks: for this is the will of God in Christ Jesus concerning you."* –1 Thessalonians 5:18.

- i) This verse is used by many to teach or believe that God is the one who uses bad things to teach them. Nothing can be further from the truth.

- ii) This verse says that we should give thanks **in** everything, not **for** everything.

   - It is not saying that we accept and embrace the bad things that happen to us as if they are from God.

- iii) The will of God is not everything. Everything we go through is not God's will but giving thanks is His will.

b) *"And said, Naked came I out of my mother's womb, and naked shall I return thither: the LORD gave, and the LORD hath taken away; blessed be the name of the LORD."* –Job 1:21.

- i) This is another verse that people use to push a teaching and belief that God uses bad things to teach us and perfect us. Again, nothing can be further from the truth.

GOT QUESTIONS?

      ii) We have to read this verse in the light of John 10:10–What Job said versus what Jesus said. Jesus' revelation (John 10:10) is superior to Job's faulty reasoning (Job 1:21).

      iii) What Job said was based on the limited knowledge of God's nature he had at that time.

- Although Job's heart was right, what he said was not a true description of the nature of God. God doesn't give and take away. He doesn't take away to teach us or perfect us.

c) *"Submit yourselves therefore to God. Resist the devil, and he will flee from you."* –James 4:7.

      i) If problems come from God to perfect us, then why do we have to resist anything? Why don't we just embrace sickness, disease, death, divorce, loss, destruction, you name it, so that we can be perfected?

      ii) Satan comes to steal, kill and destroy. We must resist anything that comes to steal, kill and destroy. How would you learn anything if you were killed?

- Sure, if we survive all these things, we can learn a thing or two, but the primary reason that all those bad things from Satan show up is to wipe us out entirely. Thank God for Jesus that we can survive many of these things.

      iii) Fight your problems. Do not embrace them. Resist the devil and he shall flee from you.

d) *"My brethren, count it all joy when ye fall into divers temptations; Knowing this, that the trying of your faith worketh patience."* –James 1:2-3.

      i) When most people read these two verses, they interpret them to mean, "God is the one who tries us through problems and temptation in order to perfect us."

- This is very misleading and gives room to many weird doctrines such as *God is the one who allows and brings problems in our lives in order to teach and perfect us.*

ii) These verses do not say God is the author of our hardships, temptations, and bad things in order to teach us (James 1:13-14 *"Let no man say when he is tempted, I am tempted of God: for God cannot be tempted with evil, neither tempteth he any man: But every man is tempted, when he is drawn away of his own lust, and enticed."*)

- God does not bring these bad things upon us, but is with us all the time, even in the midst of it. Therefore, there is a reason to rejoice.

iii) The word *"worketh"* used here comes from a Greek word which means "to *work fully,* that is, *accomplish*; by implication to *finish, fashion:* - cause, do (deed), perform, work (out)." (Strong's Concordance).

- This word further explains and means to mature and to develop not to produce. Temptations, problems, and tragedies do not produce patience (faith sustained over a long period of time), nor teach and perfect us. It is wrong to try to embrace these things in order to become patient. They will instead destroy you.

iv) What temptations, problems, and hardships do is that they give us opportunity to exercise, mature and develop our patience, but they do not produce it and they do not come from God.

e) *"But the fruit of the Spirit is love, joy, peace, longsuffering **patience**, gentleness, goodness, faith, Meekness, temperance self-control: against such there is no law."* –Galatians 5:22-23 (emphasis mine).

Patience, learning, and maturity is produced from and by the Word of God, not from problems, tribulation, and hardships. Patience is also a fruit of the Spirit (Galatians 5:22-23).

i) *"For whatsoever things were written aforetime were written for our learning, that we through patience and comfort of the Scriptures might have hope."* –Romans 15:4.

ii) *"So then faith cometh by hearing, and hearing by the Word of God."* –Romans 10:17.

f) *"And we know that all things work together for good to them that love God, to them who are the called according to his purpose."* –Romans 8:28.

    i) This verse does not say, *"All things come from God to work together for good,"* yet many people read this verse like that. Then they end up saying that God allows, and/or causes problems to come into our lives in order to teach us.

    ii) This verse does not also say that whatever happens to us works out for our own good. Problems, bad things, tragedies, and hardships do not come from God nor does He allow or will them to mature, teach and perfect us.

        ○ At least that is not how God does it. Again, although some people might learn through their experience, that is not the way God teaches us (2 Timothy 3:16-17).

    iii) What this verse is saying is that because we love God and are called according to His purpose, He will intervene in any situation and turn it around in our favor.

        ○ When the enemy brings destruction, tragedy and problems unto us, God will come in and redeem that situation on our behalf.

g) *"There hath no temptation taken you but such as is common to man: but God is faithful, who will not suffer you to be tempted above that ye are able; but will with the temptation also make a way to escape, that ye may be able to bear it."* –1 Corinthians 10:13.

Chapter Thirteen

i) Some people have taken this verse to say that the Lord is the one who brings temptations, hardships, and bad things into our lives and that this is His promise that He will not put on us more than we can bear. That is not so. This interpretation goes against James 1:13-14.

ii) This verse is not saying that the Lord causes or allows these temptations, hardships, sickness to come into our lives. It is just saying that God will not let temptations and hardships to overtake us. If those limits are reached, He will make a way of escape.

How then does God teach us?

There are multiple ways we can learn and change. Many have believed that **the only** way we learn is through experience, hence the phrase "Experience is the best teacher." Nothing can be further from the truth! I will show you multiple ways I believe through which we can learn, be taught, and experience change and growth which will include experience.

There are two primary ways we learn and experience change. We have a choice as to how we want to learn.

a) Light–Light is in reference to revelation. This revelation comes through a few ways:

   o The Word–Psalm 119:130, *"The entrance of thy words giveth light; it giveth understanding unto the simple."*

   o The Holy Spirit.

b) Heat–This is the school of hard knocks or hardships. This is bush university. I remember President Ronald Regan said that, *"When you can't make them see the light, make them feel the heat."* Heat is an option to learn and change although it is not the best option. The best option is light.

GOT QUESTIONS?

1. The Word of God

    God's discipline for His children is always one-on-one and always involves His Word, not a sickness, disease, natural disaster, or tragedy. Here are Scriptures that show you how God teaches His children (2 Timothy 3:16-17; 1 Peter 2:2; 1 Corinthians 10:6-11; John 14:26; John 15:1-3; Joshua 1:8; Ephesians 4:11-13; 6:17; Psalm 34:11; 94:12; 119:9-11,103,105,133; Hebrews 4:2; John 15:1-3; Rev 3:16-17).

    "All Scripture is given by inspiration of God, and is profitable for doctrine, for reproof, for correction, for instruction in righteousness: That the man of God may be perfect, thoroughly furnished unto all good works."

    −2 Timothy 3:16-17

    a) Able to make you wise unto salvation

        i) God's word is and has the wisdom of God and is able to make us wise. We should take it seriously and humble ourselves and receive it, for it is able to save our souls (James 1:21). Humility means agreeing with God, depending on God, and doing what God has said.

    b) Reproof

        i) The Greek word for *"reproof"* in this verse means *"proof, conviction"* (Strong's Concordance).

        ii) God's word brings conviction. True conviction comes from God's word. Conviction is not the same as condemnation. Conviction helps us change and become better, but condemnation says we can't change. Condemnation says you can't change but conviction won't let you stay the same. God's word is the chief agent for change in our lives.

Chapter Thirteen

c) Correction

 i) The Greek word for "correction" in this verse means "a straightening up again, that is, (figuratively) rectification (reformation)" (Strong's Concordance).

 ii) God's word will help correct us when we go astray. Judgment does not necessarily bring correction, but God has chosen to use His word to correct us. God always uses His word to correct us and He always does it one-on-one not corporately.

d) Instruction in righteousness

 i) The Greek word for "instruction" used in this verse means "tutorage, that is, education or training; by implication disciplinary correction" (Strong's Concordance).

 ii) True training and education must have its roots, foundation and basis on God's word. We need it to train our children in the way they should go (Proverbs 22:6).

e) Make you perfect

 i) The Greek word for *"perfect"* used in this verse means *"fresh,* that is, (by implication) *complete"* (Strong's Concordance).

 ii) We cannot be complete without God's word. God's word will make us mature and complete.

f) Thoroughly furnished unto all good works

 i) The Greek word for "furnished" used in this verse means "to finish out (time); figuratively to equip fully" (Strong's Concordance).

 ii) God's Word will fully equip us to live a godly life and be fruitful in all things.

GOT QUESTIONS?

Clean through the Word

"I am the true vine, and my Father is the husbandman. Every branch in me that beareth not fruit he taketh away: and every branch that beareth fruit, he purgeth it, that it may bring forth more fruit. Now ye are clean through the word which I have spoken unto you."

–John 15:1-3

i) The word *"purgeth"* comes from a Greek word translated "to *cleanse*, that is, (specifically) to *prune*; figuratively to *expiate:* -purge." (Strong's Concordance).

- So this is talking about cleansing and pruning.

ii) I have heard some people teach and use this verse as a precedent for how God teaches us.

- They say that God must purge and prune us by problems, sickness, death, poverty or misery so that we can bear more fruit which is a painful process.
- This kind of thinking leaves an impression that hardship, tragedies, sicknesses, bad things and so forth are all good things and it leads many people to embrace these things instead of rejecting and resisting them (James 4:7).
- It also paints a false picture that there is no bearing fruit without these problems and bad things.

iii) However, if you read verse 3, you will see that it tells us exactly how God purges, prunes, and cleanses us.

- He does so through His Word, not through hardships, sickness, death, poverty or bad things that happen to us.
- True, some might learn through those hardships, tragedies, and bad things, but it is inaccurate to teach or believe that God uses those things to teach us.

Chapter Thirteen

- If your choice of learning was the school of hard knocks, do not blame God for your choice of learning because His choice is through and by His word.

iv) God does not use tools of the devil to mature, develop and perfect His children. He uses His word.

v) The irony of thinking that God is the one who does these things to us in order to teach us simply means that we should not resist these things if we are to be consistent with our thoughts or belief system.

- For example, you shouldn't go to the doctor if it is sickness that perfects, matures and grows us. If you do go to the doctor, you are just a hypocrite. You are going against "God's way" of teaching us. Why don't you let cancer mature and better you? Do you see how nonsensical this is?

Teaches him out of Thy law

"Blessed is the man whom thou chastenest, O LORD, and teachest him out of thy law;"

–Psalm 94:12

i) The law of the Lord is also referred to as the Word of God. It is through this that God teaches and chastens us. Teaching that God does it through tragedy or hardship is not the truth. Teach us through Thy word, oh Lord.

Cleanse his way

"Wherewithal shall a young man cleanse his way? by taking heed thereto according to thy word. With my whole heart have I sought thee: O let me not wander from thy commandments. Thy word have I hid in mine heart, that I might not sin against thee." [104-105] *Through thy precepts I get understanding: therefore, I hate*

every false way. Thy word is a lamp unto my feet, and a light unto my path. ¹³³ *Order my steps in thy word: and let not any iniquity have dominion over me."*

—Psalm 119:9-11, 104-105, 133

i) The way we can cleanse our ways is by and through the word of God. Understanding, completion, maturity comes from the word of God.

ii) God's word gives us guidance and enlightenment, which helps us to mature. It is through His word that He orders and directs our paths and ways.

iii) Notice that these verses say nothing about the problems or tragedies as ways in which God teaches us. There is no growth, learning and maturity outside of God's word. We need God's word for growth to occur (1 Peter 2:2).

Milk of the Word

"As newborn babes, desire the sincere milk of the word, that ye may grow thereby:"

—1 Peter 2:2

i) Growth comes from the word of God, not problems, tragedies, hardships or bad things that happen to us. Just as babes grow by milk, we grow by and mature through the word of God by the help of the Holy Spirit.

Thy way prosperous

"This book of the law shall not depart out of thy mouth; but thou shalt meditate therein day and night, that thou mayest observe to do according to all that is written therein: for then thou shalt make thy way prosperous, and then thou shalt have good success."

—Joshua 1:8

i) The book of the law is another way of saying the word of God.

ii) This Scripture teaches that it is through the word of God that we make our ways prosperous and have good success. Like many other passages of scripture, this one also clearly emphasizes that the word of God is the key to prospering, maturing, and increase.

iii) As we begin to meditate on God's word, we begin to develop and experience success, increase, and maturity.

Chastisement

"And ye have forgotten the exhortation which speaketh unto you as unto children, My son, despise not thou the chastening of the Lord, nor faint when thou art rebuked of him: For whom the Lord loveth he chasteneth, and scourgeth every son whom he receiveth. If ye endure chastening, God dealeth with you as with sons; for what son is he whom the father chasteneth not? But if ye be without chastisement, whereof all are partakers, then are ye bastards, and not sons. Furthermore, we have had fathers of our flesh which corrected us, and we gave them reverence: shall we not much rather be in subjection unto the Father of spirits, and live?"

– Hebrews 12:5-9

i) Contrary to what most people take from this verse, God does not chasten us with sickness, problems, tragedy, or bad things. This is not true.

ii) The word *"chastening"* comes from a Greek word translated: "*tutorage, that is, education* or *training*; by implication disciplinary *correction:* - chastening, chastisement, instruction, nurture" (Strong's Concordance) AND *"chasteneth"* comes from a Greek word that mean "*train* up a child, that is, *educate*, or (by implication) *discipline* (by punishment): - chasten (-ise), instruct, learn, teach." (Strong's Concordance).

iii) We see clearly that these verses are talking about God correcting, educating, training (like training up a child), and instructing.

- This is exactly what 2 Timothy 3:16-17 teaches. God does His teaching to us through His Word, not through problems, bad things, and tragedy.

2. Revelation knowledge.

We can also learn and change by receiving revelation knowledge from God and the word.

a) Galatians 1:12, For I neither received it of man, neither was I taught it, but by the revelation of Jesus Christ.

b) 1 Samuel 3:21, And the Lord appeared again in Shiloh: for the Lord revealed himself to Samuel in Shiloh by the word of the Lord.

3. Holy Spirit

The scriptures also teach clearly that the Holy Spirit is our teacher. He wants to teach us all things.

But the Comforter, which is the Holy Ghost, whom the Father will send in my name, he shall teach you all things, and bring all things to your remembrance, whatsoever I have said unto you.

–John 14:26

Howbeit when he, the Spirit of truth, is come, he will guide you into all truth: for he shall not speak of himself; but whatsoever he shall hear, that shall he speak: and he will show you things to come.

–John 16:13

a) He will teach them ALL THINGS and bring all things to their remembrance. Notice He did not say that He will teach us a few or some things, but all things.

b) No tragedy, problem or hardship can teach us all things. Only the Holy Spirit can through the word of God. Although, we all will learn from the bad things that happen to us, God does not teach us that way. It is just another way we choose to learn.

c) Notice that this verse does not say that He will bring tragedies, problems, and bad things to teach us, but He will teach us through the Holy Spirit.

d) The Holy Spirit is the Author of the Word of God (2 Timothy 3:16-17). He teaches us by pointing us to the word and expounding on it to give us understanding.

But the anointing which ye have received of him abideth in you, and ye need not that any man teach you: but as the same anointing teacheth you of all things, and is truth, and is no lie, and even as it hath taught you, ye shall abide in him.

—1 John 2:27

a) This is saying that we are not limited to a human teacher. If we were alone on the earth or even in jail and had no human teacher, we could be taught of the Lord through the Holy Spirit who lives on the inside of us.

b) This is not saying that no one will teach you ANYTHING.

c) In context, "all things" is talking about those who deny that Jesus is the Christ and were seducing others to believe the same.

d) Paul was not taught of man but of the Lord (Galatians 1:11-12).

4. Fivefold Ministry Office Gifts

"And he gave some, apostles; and some, prophets; and some, evangelists; and some, pastors and teachers; For the perfecting of the saints, for the work of the ministry, for the edifying of the body of Christ: Till we all come in the unity of the faith, and of the knowledge of the Son of God, unto a perfect man, unto the measure of the stature of the fullness of Christ:"

—Ephesians 4:11-13

a) When God wrote these scriptures, He forgot to say that problems, hardships, sufferings, and bad things would edify, mature and perfect the body of Christ, right? wrong!

   i) These verses teach that we are given the fivefold ministry to help edify, mature, teach and perfect the body of Christ. The Lord did not give problems, hardships and tragedy as means for us to learn, grow, and mature.

5. Experience

    Although some have believed that experience is the best teacher, it is the most expensive, and it is not always the best teacher. I'm not trying to disregard experience, but I'm rather trying to put it in the right perspective. Experience has to be evaluated for us to learn from it. Experience alone is not the best teacher.

    In life, sometimes we win and sometimes we learn–not lose. We need to learn from the bad experiences and let them go. You can either focus on the loss, lesson, and/or the cross.

    There are many people that have experience, yet they did not learn or change a thing, and some learn only the negative things such as not to trust, not to have high expectations, and so forth. Not all experiences teach as some have believed, but if it does, for one to learn and change through his experience, they have to want to learn and they should believe and trust God in that process as He is the best teacher.

    a) Personal Experience

        Every past success or failure we experience can be a valuable source of direction, information, and wisdom. Success teaches us what we can do and gives us confidence.

        And Laban said unto him, I pray thee, if I have found favor in thine eyes, tarry: for I have learned by experience that the LORD hath blessed me for thy sake.

        – Genesis 30:27

    i)   Laban mentions that he learned that the Lord had blessed him because of Jacob. This learning was by experience. He learned by experience.

b)   Experience of others

> *Now these things were our examples, to the intent we should not lust after evil things, as they also lusted. Neither be ye idolaters, as were some of them; as it is written, The people sat down to eat and drink, and rose up to play. Neither let us commit fornication, as some of them committed, and fell in one day three and twenty thousand. Neither let us tempt Christ, as some of them also tempted, and were destroyed of serpents. Neither murmur ye, as some of them also murmured, and were destroyed of the destroyer. Now all these things happened unto them for examples: and they are written for our admonition, upon whom the ends of the world are come.*
>
> —1 Corinthians 10:6-11

These verses teach that things in the Old Testament were written for our examples and admonition. In other words, this is saying that we can learn through another person's experience. We can learn at the expense of those written in the scriptures.

We do not have to go through bad things and hardships that others have gone through. We do not have to attend the same school of hard knocks nor the university of hardships. We can use the written word as an example and learn.

We can see the things that happened to the other people, learn, grow, and mature. We do not have to embrace their hardships. I believe that although people say experience is a good teacher, I believe that experience from the word of God is the best teacher.

    i)   We can learn and change through and by the example and the experience of others. The word of God lists many examples, both good and bad of those who walked before us. One of the reasons it lists those examples is so we can learn from them and change.

ii) We should not disregard other people's experiences in order to experience things ourselves. That is a sick mindset. If we look at things this way, many of us will not be around to see the fruit of those experiences. We do not have to make the mistakes ourselves to learn from them. Wisdom teaches us to avoid those mistakes by observing and learning the right lessons gleaned from other people.

In conclusion, it is trusting the Lord and studying the word that makes us stronger and better. Problems are not from God, but He does help us navigate through them if we let Him.

Chapter Fourteen

What is Free Will?

Free will can be defined as an inidividual's volition and capacity to make decisions and choices (regardless of the results) without any external constraints or pressure. It reveals that God gives humans the opportunity to make choices that genuinely affect their destiny. Although we have a free will, it doesn't come without some limitations. There are things about our life that we did not get to choose. We didn't choose our parents, our skin color, or country of origin, and so on. *But by the grace of God, we have the ability to exercise our free will to choose salvation while in our sinful nature.*

We were created in the image of God with the capacity to choose God. Every time you make a choice, you are exercising your free will. God will not violate the power of your choice. That is His choice. Although we have a free will, we should choose right and wisely. Choosing to follow the Lord is the wise and right choice (Deuteronomy 30:19).

Everything that God has provided for us by grace has to be received through our free will. Nothing is forced on us. We must choose to receive what God has chosen to give us freely. Every decision we make in life is a choice. Many times, we make wrong choices and then blame God for them.

A choice hasn't been made if there still remains an option. The reason people fall away is because they have not chosen to follow the Lord. For me I have decided and I'm intentional at making my decisions upfront, not as I go. Making decisions as I go opens me up to too much error. It's best to seek the Lord and find out His heart and make a decision to follow that and go that way.

Choices require declarations (2 Corinthians 4:13). When you declare and speak forth your choice, you will establish that thing through the law of life and death through the power of the tongue (Proverbs 18:21). You will be committed to something that you choose and declare. If you do not choose your choices and declare them with your mouth, you will still have room for wavering. If you have not made a choice, you will waver (James 1:6-8). It is important to use your free will in an honorable and godly manner. When you make your choice and declare it loud in your words, you will hardly break it, or even be tempted with another. Therefore, it is important that we make the right choices. Every choice is an affirmation of one thing and a denial of another. Every choice is a seed which carries within it the harvest of its nature.

Free will is one of the best gifts God gave man. We can choose whatever we want. We can choose what to eat, what to wear, what to buy - on and on the list goes. When God created man, He gave him a free will, or what some call, the right to choose. God did not create robots which He controls and manipulates the way He wants. He created human beings, and in the garden, He gave Adam and Eve the freedom to eat from any tree except the tree of the Knowledge of good and evil.

"I call heaven and earth to record this day against you, that I have set before you life and death, blessing and cursing: therefore choose life, that both thou and thy seed may live:"

–Deuteronomy 30:19

Every man created has a free will to choose life or death, heaven or hell, light or darkness, Jesus or Satan. People say that if God is a good God, why does He send people to hell? Nothing can be further from the truth. If I gave you an option to choose life or death and I also give you guidance to choose the right thing (life), but you rebel against me and exercise your right to choose death, why would you blame me for the consequences of your choice? People choose death and hell. God doesn't send them there. They choose to go there and because God gave each man the freedom to choose as they will, God has a responsibility to let people have what they choose. He respects their choice. He doesn't change His word and say, "Oops, you made a wrong decision, I command you to choose this or that." No, it doesn't work like that.

The verses below teach that we have a free will, which is seen through our choices;

a) *"And unto this people thou shalt say, Thus saith the LORD; Behold, I set before you the way of life, and the way of death."* –Jeremiah 21:8.

b) *"When your fear cometh as desolation, and your destruction cometh as a whirlwind; when distress and anguish cometh upon you. Then shall they call upon me, but I will not answer; they shall seek me early, but they shall not find me: For that they hated knowledge, and **did not choose the fear of the Lord**:"*–Proverbs 1:27-29 (Emphasis mine)..

c) *"Let thine hand help me; for **I have chosen** thy precepts."*–Psalm 119:173 (Emphasis mine).

d) *"Know ye not, that to whom ye yield yourselves servants to obey, his servants ye are to whom ye obey; whether of sin unto death, or of obedience unto righteousness?"* –Romans 6:16

In conclusion, with free will comes responsibility. We have a free will and therefore have the responsibility of making the wise and right choices. If we do not, then we suffer the consequences that come from our wrong choices (Galatians 6:7-8).

What does it mean to be born again?

*"Jesus answered and said unto him, Verily, verily, I say unto thee, Except a man be **born again**, he cannot see the kingdom of God."* (Emphasis mine).

–John 3:3

GOT QUESTIONS?

To be born again simply means to believe and receive Jesus Christ into your heart believing that He died on the cross for your sins and was raised from the dead (Romans 10:9-10). Those who are born again are in relationship with God, which only comes through faith in Jesus. It also referred to as:

a) To be saved (Romans 10:9-10)
b) To be reconciled to God (Romans 5:10; 2 Corinthians 5:20).
c) To be forgiven (Ephesians 1:7 and Colossians 1:14).
d) To be called out of darkness into the Kingdom of His Dear Son (Colossians 1:13).
e) A new creature (2 Corinthians 5:17).
f) To be in Christ (2 Corinthians 5:17).
g) To be regenerated (Titus 3:5).
h) Believing on the Lord (Acts 16:31).
i) Receiving Jesus (John 1:12; Colossians 2:6).
j) Repenting and turning to Jesus (Acts 26:20; Acts 3:19).
k) Conversion (Acts 3:19).
l) To be born of God (1 John 5:1, 4, 18).
m) To be born of the Spirit (John 3:5, 6, 8).
n) To be sons of God (Romans 8:14).
o) Baptism in the body of Christ (1 Corinthians 12:13).
p) To have a new spirit (Ezekiel 36:26).
q) To have a new heart (Ezekiel 36:26).
r) Washed, made holy, made righteous and justified (1 Corinthians 6:11).
s) To have a divine nature (2 Peter 1:4).
t) Eternal life or relationship with God through Christ Jesus (John 3:16; 17:3).

Accepting Jesus into your heart that He died and rose again is the best decision you could and would ever make. It will change your life in this life, and in the life to come. God wants to have a personal relationship with you.

Here is an opportunity to receive and accept Jesus into your heart. Deciding to receive Jesus Christ as your Lord and Savior is the most important decision you'll ever make! Nothing comes close to this decision; not your career and

Chapter Fourteen

not your spouse. God loved you and I so much that He took it upon Himslef to pay the price for our own sins by sending Jesus to die on the cross. He did this because He loved you and I so much. How do you know that Jesus loves you? It is because He died for you. Only a person that loves you would be willing to die for you. How could I doubt the love of one who gave up everything and died for me? It would be very sad for me to teach you that Jesus was and is God and not give you an opportunity to repent and to receive Him into your heart as your Lord and Savior. Will you accept Him as God, not just another good man like some believe and say?

God has promised, "That if thou shalt confess with thy mouth the Lord Jesus, and shalt believe in thine heart that God hath raised him from the dead, thou shalt be saved. For with the heart man believeth unto righteousness; and with the mouth confession is made unto salvation.... For whosoever shall call upon the name of the Lord shall be saved" (Rom. 10:9-10, 13).

By His grace, God has already done everything to provide for your salvation. Your part is simply to believe and receive. It is the easiest decision. This is a heart decision, not a head decision. Now is the acceptable time, today is the day of salvation (2 Cor. 6:2). *Why wait?*

Pray this prayer and mean it sincerely from your heart:

Jesus, I confess that You are my Lord and Savior. I believe in my heart that God raised You from the dead. By faith in Your Word, I receive salvation now. Thank You for saving me!

The very moment you commit your life to Jesus Christ, the truth of His word instantly comes to pass in your spirit. Now that you're born again and you are a new creation, though you may not feel any different. You have the Spirit of God living inside of you and He will talk to you and teach you about your brand new life. God has created in you a new spirit and a new heart.

Chapter Fifteen

Is Hell a Reality, a Myth or a Metaphor?

Many people have received the Gospel with open hands, and they should. However, many have gone overboard and have ended up in deception instead. They have lost the balance of the Gospel and have started to believe that there is no longer a hell. The truth is that there is a hell for all those who do not accept God's grace.

The Gospel is the "too good to be true news", but it is not good news to proclaim that people are going to hell. By sharing the good news of the Gospel, we can draw more bees with honey than with vinegar. Romans 2:4, *"Or do you despise the riches of His goodness, forbearance, and longsuffering, not knowing that the goodness of God leads you to repentance?"* (NKJV) It is the goodness of God that leads men to repentance, not the wrath of God.

I have been gravely troubled by the waves of doctrine that are hitting the church such as ultimate reconciliation, universalism and that a good God cannot send people to hell. These wrong teachings and doctrines teach that God will ultimately reconcile all people to Himself, which includes the devil and all of the people in hell. Additionally, some say that hell is not real and that it is a state of mind and not a real place. They say that if hell does exist, it is just for a temporary and limited point of time. How wrong can something be!

If we can only understand what God delivered us from, we will be forever grateful to God for His goodness. Because we all owed a debt that we could never pay, Jesus paid for the sins of the whole world (2 Corinthians 5:19 and 1 John 2:2). He did not just speak words, change His thoughts about sin or look the other way, saying, "it's fine. People do not have to go to hell."

Jesus paid for our sins so we should never have to go there. However, those who reject or ignore such a great sacrifice will forever pay for their sins for all eternity (2 Thessalonians 1:8-10).

Jesus took the judgment of sin because sin needed to be judged. Romans 6:23, *"For the wages of sin is death, but the gift of God is eternal life in Christ Jesus our Lord."*

"Who Himself bore our sins in His own body on the tree, that we, having died to sins, might live for righteousness–by whose stripes you were healed."

–1 Peter 2:24

You see, according to John 16:8-9 *"And when he is come, he will reprove the world of sin, and of righteousness, and of judgment: Of sin, because they believe not on me;,* the issue is not the individual sins that we have committed but the ultimate sin (singular) of rejecting Jesus' sacrifice and payment for our sins. The only sin people go to hell for is not murder, theft, rape, on and on the list goes. Jesus paid for all these sins. Those sins cannot send you to hell but the sin of rejecting Jesus' sacrifice for all your sins will.

If I decided to pay for all the things you owe (debt) in life, your only responsibility would be to say yes, receive, and accept my payments for you. If you rejected my payment for whatever I have paid for you, then you will pay for those things I have already paid for. You have lost or you will work to pay for what is already piad for the rest of your life.

Jesus' sacrifice that He made on the cross is infinitely greater than the sins we have committed. He actually overpaid for our sins and He didn't mind it. God became sin so that we can become the very righteousness of God. There was an exchange–His righteousness for our sins. He was also forsaken because He became sin (Matthew 27:46). Those who reject Jesus' sacrifice for their sins as their Lord and Savior will face a real hell.

Chapter Fifteen

Luke 16:22-26a, *"And it came to pass, that the beggar died, and was carried by the angels into Abraham's bosom: the rich man also died, and was buried; And in hell he lift up his eyes, being in torments, and seeth Abraham afar off, and Lazarus in his bosom. And he cried and said, Father Abraham, have mercy on me, and send Lazarus, that he may dip the tip of his finger in water, and cool my tongue; for I am tormented in this flame. But Abraham said, Son, remember that thou in thy lifetime receivedst thy good things, and likewise Lazarus evil things: but now he is comforted and thou art tormented. And beside all this, between us and you there is a great gulf fixed."*

a) This was not a fairytale that Jesus was telling. This was a real story that Jesus used to speak about hell. Jesus was not making things up or lying.

b) The rich man spoke to Abraham from hell, the place of torment.

c) It makes it clear that in *sheol*, or hell, those who were in torment could see those across the gulf.

d) The rich man in hell never died. He could hear, thirst, feel pain and sorrow, and even communicate with Lazarus in paradise.

e) God sees differently from the way the world does. The rich man that this world would be honoring was found wanting by God and the poor man who would have been considered a nobody and despised was greatly honored by the Lord. The key was not their wealth, but their faith in Jesus. One was found wanting while the other (Lazarus) had made the right decision.

f) We can also see from Scripture that there are no second chances. There is no purgatory, as Catholicism teaches. There is no ultimate reconciliation and no universalism (For more detail refer to "What about universal salvation?" chapter two in this book). On earth, the rich man rejected God and went directly to hell. When the rich man pleaded for mercy, Abraham could do nothing. There will be no mercy, no hope, and no goodness of any kind in hell, ever.

GOT QUESTIONS?

According to Hebrews 9:27, "And as it is appointed unto men once to die, but after this the judgment:" you have ONE chance. You must take that chance in this life.

Hell is an awful, gross, terrible place where no one should want to go, and I believe that explains why people oppose its existence by hiding behind the grace and the goodness of God. Hell was never prepared for man, but *"for the devil and his angels"* (Matthew 25:41). However, Isaiah 5:14 says that hell has enlarged herself to make room for those who choose to go there, and it is now never full (Proverbs 27:20).

Jesus did the hard work by becoming man, dying on the cross and paying the price of sin for mankind. Our part is the easiest–just to believe on and receive Jesus' sacrifice for ourselves. I tell you, for people to go to hell, they have to work so much at it.

God has placed roadblocks across our path, barriers, obstructions and even mountains, to stop people from going to hell, but people still climb over them and do anything to get their way to hell.

Someone once said, there is no atheist on a deathbed. All of a sudden, they begin to think about life after this life, or hell.

> *"There are only two kinds of people in the end: those who say to God, "Thy will be done" and those to whom God says, in the end, "Thy will be done." All that are in Hell choose it."*
>
> –C.S. Lewis, The Great Divorce

Not one of us can earn their way into relationship with God. There is no good act or good deed that any man can do to gain favor with God. True, you might be better than me, but according to the bible, all have sinned and come short of the glory of God (Romans 3:23). There is not a hell number two or a hell number three. Even if you are better than your neighbor, you have still failed and your self-righteousness is like filthy rags before God, according to Isaiah 64:6. If it were possible to earn your righteousness and right standing with God, there would be no need for Jesus to come and die for the sins of the whole world.

Chapter Fifteen

In the Old Testament, the Hebrew word *sheol* was translated "hell" thirty-one times and "grave" thirty-one times. Nearly every time it's translated "grave," it's talking about where the godly go after death, and when it's translated "hell," it's talking about the destination of the ungodly.

The word "hell" appears 54 times in the Holy Bible. Hell is clearly defined in your bible as a place of torment, darkness, weeping and gnashing of teeth, sorrows, deep pain, devouring everlasting fire, and everlasting burning. There is no party in hell.

Hell is real and you do not what to find that out after getting there because there is no way back. If you have not made Jesus your personal Lord and savior, make that right decision today and receive Jesus into your heart as your personal Lord and Savior (Romans 10:9-10).

Chapter Sixteen

Why Do I Have to Go to Church if God is Everywhere?

One day I asked my colleague this question and he responded, "You do not have to go to church!" I have come to understand that sometimes people do things out of obligation including going to church. You do not have to go to church. You **get** to go to church. Huge difference! I need to point out that "church" is not speaking about a building but the believers whether in a building or not. There are so many benefits to going to a gathering of believers. In addition to that, we can learn from the example of the scriptures. What does the Bible teach?

"Let us hold fast the profession of our faith without wavering; (for he is faithful that promised;) And let us consider one another to provoke unto love and to good works: Not forsaking the assembling of ourselves together, as the manner of some is; but exhorting one another: and so much the more, as ye see the day approaching."

–Hebrews 10:23-25

These scriptures tell us not to forsake gathering together as some people want to do or have decided to do. It also goes on and outlines some of the benefits of gathering together, such as:

A. Encouraging one another

   a) We get encouraged when we spend time with fellow believers

b) *"But exhort one another daily, while it is called To day; lest any of you be hardened through the deceitfulness of sin."*- Hebrews 3:13. While we can encourage one another via email, text, phone call or social media, it is very beneficial to come together and communicate one-on-one while edifying, sharpening one another, rubbing shoulders with one another, talking together in person, receiving hugs, sharing meals together.

c) You will also receive prayer and you will be encouraged and built up by fellow believers.

B. Provoke each other unto love and good works

a) *"And let us consider one another to provoke unto love and to good works:"* –Hebrews 10:24

i) If we are going to achieve this, we want to come together in one place and gather.

C. God's will

a) It is God's will for us to be gathering. This verse (Hebrews 10:23-25) is clearly against the notion that most people encourage against not going to church. Notice it says, *"NOT forsaking the assembling of ourselves together."*

D. Flourish

a) *"Those that be planted in the house of the Lord shall flourish in the courts of our God."* –Psalm 92:13

E. Fellowship

a) We grow better together than alone. No man is an island. We need each other. We were created for fellowship. Two are better than one! (Ecclesiastes 4:9). When we go to church, you will make new friends, lifelong friends and connections.

Chapter Sixteen

    i) *"And they continued stedfastly in the apostles' doctrine and fellowship, and in breaking of bread, and in prayers." –Acts 2:42*

    ii) You will get an opportunity to minister to others and touch lives. You can't effectively do this on your couch without going to the people.

    iii) Going to church will open an opportunity for you to take a friend who might eventually come to accept the Lord.

F. Worship

"For where two or three are gathered together in my name, there am I in the midst of them."

–Matthew 18:20

    a) Corporate worship is powerful (Colossians 3:16).

G. Opportunity to serve

    a) You will be able to discover and put your God-given giftings to work. You will discover your calling and purpose.

H. Sign of Commitment to the Lord

It shows your commitment to the Lord and it honors Him since He Himself gathered with the people constantly. As a matter of fact, we see examples of people in scripture going to church, the temple, or synagogue:

    a) Jesus

        i) *"And Jesus went about all Galilee, teaching in their synagogues, and preaching the Gospel of the kingdom, and healing all manner of sickness and all manner of disease among the people."–Matthew 4:23; Matthew 9:35*

        ii) There was an aspect of gathering together for edification.

      iii) *"And it came to pass, that after three days they found him in the temple, sitting in the midst of the doctors, both hearing them, and asking them questions."*–Luke 2:46

  b) Peter and John

      i) *"Who seeing Peter and John about to go into the temple asked an alms."* –Acts 3:3

  c) Disciples met on the first day of the week

      i) *"And upon the first day of the week, when the disciples came together to break bread, Paul preached unto them, ready to depart on the morrow; and continued his speech until midnight."* –Acts 20:7

      ii) *"Upon the first day of the week let every one of you lay by him in store, as God hath prospered him, that there be no gatherings when I come."* –1 Corinthians 16:2

      iii) *"For the body is not one member, but many."* –1 Corinthians 12:14

- Many times, the legs come to church, but the hands stayed home, the eyes came to church, but the liver stayed in bed, the ears came to church, but the fingers are holding the TV remote control. This is not functioning as a body. We need to be together as a body - complete. For a church body to be functioning together well, all members must be present. In addition, all these members should be involved in some type of ministry to others and put to use their spiritual gifts.

1. Come together in one place

    Lastly, as we read the Word of God, we find this phrase *"come in one place"* or *"come together in one place"* repeated multiple times. The use of these phrases is emphasizing the need to gather together as a body for worship and fellowship. We cannot come together in one place while some have stayed home.

Chapter Sixteen

"If therefore the whole church be come together into one place, and all speak with tongues, and there come in those that are unlearned, or unbelievers, will they not say that ye are mad?"

—1 Corinthians 14:23

"When ye come together therefore into one place, this is not to eat the Lord's supper."

—1 Corinthians 11:20

"How is it then, brethren? When ye come together, every one of you hath a psalm, hath a doctrine, hath a tongue, hath a revelation, hath an interpretation. Let all things be done unto edifying."

—1 Corinthians 14:26

Church (assembly of believers) is not just about what you receive, but also what you impart to others. The best way to impart unto others is in person. Ephesians 4:15-16 make it clear that speaking the truth in love causes us to grow up in all things. This happens most effectively when we come together on a regular basis.

Church is opportunity for iron sharpening iron. Proverbs 27:17 says *"Iron sharpeneth iron; so a man sharpeneth the countenance of his friend."* We cannot sharpen each other without coming together.

Receive Jesus As Your Savior

Deciding to receive Jesus Christ as your Lord and Savior is the most important decision you'll ever make! Nothing comes close to this decision; not your career and not even your spouse. It will change your life now and your eternal destiny. There is no decision that could be made that is like it. It would be very sad for me to teach you that Jesus was and is God and not give you an opportunity to repent and to receive Him into your heart as your God and Savior. Will you accept Him as God and not just another good man like some believe and say?

God has promised, *"If thou shalt confess with thy mouth the Lord Jesus, and shalt believe in thine heart that God hath raised him from the dead, thou shalt be saved. For with the heart man believeth unto righteousness; and with the mouth confession is made unto salvation.... For whosoever shall call upon the name of the Lord shall be saved."* (Romans 10:9-10, 13).

By His grace, God has already done everything on His part to provide for your salvation. Your part is simply to believe and receive. It is the easiest decision. This is a heart decision, not a head decision. Now is the acceptable time, today is the day of salvation (2 Corinthians 6:2). Why wait?

Pray this prayer and mean it sincerely from your heart:

Lord Jesus,
I confess that You are my Lord and Savior. I believe in my heart that God raised You from the dead. By faith in Your Word, I receive salvation, now. Thank You for saving me!

The very moment you commit your life to Jesus Christ, the truth of His Word instantly comes to pass in your spirit. Now that you're born again, you are brand new on the inside. God has created in you a new spirit and a new heart.

Receive the Baptism of the Holy Spirit

Living a Christian life is not just a difficult thing to do but an impossible thing. You need help. So, because it is impossible to live a victorious, Christian life without the baptism of the Holy Spirit, the Lord wants to give you the supernatural power you need to live this new life. We receive power when we receive the baptism of the Holy Spirit (Acts 1:8).

It's as simple as asking and receiving. When we ask for the Holy Spirit, the Lord will give Him to us (Luke 11:10, 13).

All you have to do is ask, believe, and receive! Pray:

Father, I recognize my need for Your power to live this new life. Please fill me with Your Holy Spirit. By faith, I receive Him right now! Thank You for baptizing me. Holy Spirit, You are welcome in my life.

Congratulations! Now you're filled with God's supernatural power. Some syllables from a language you don't recognize will rise up from your heart to your mouth (See 1 Corinthians 14:14). Go ahead and speak those syllables. As you speak them out loud by faith, you're releasing God's power from within and building yourself up in the Spirit (See 1 Corinthians 14:4). You can do this whenever and wherever you like.

It doesn't really matter whether you felt anything or not when you prayed to receive the Lord and His Spirit. If you believed in your heart that you received, then God's Word promises that you received. ***"Therefore, I say unto you, What things soever ye desire, when ye pray, believe that ye receive them, and ye shall have them"*** (Mark 11:24). God always honors His Word–believe it!

Jesus; God or Man?

by Rich Kanyali

Paperback
ISBN: 978-1513627113
eBook is also available

In this book, Rich takes you on a journey to discover a certain truth that distinguishes Christianity from any other religion, faith, or belief system. Have you ever given a single thought as to whether Jesus was God or man?

To some, Jesus was a good man. To some, He was a great historical figure. To some, He was god (not divine). To others, an angel (Michael the Archangel). To some, a prophet, but to others, He was and is God. So, which is which? What category do you fall into? Was Jesus God or man? Within the pages of this book, you will find powerful biblical proof and sound reasoning to who Jesus truly was and is. The evidence is within the pages of this book. The truth is unveiled leaving no stone unturned. Reading this book will shed light unto your understanding and give you a greater revelation of this truth.

All books by Rich Kanyali are available on:

RichKanyali.com
Amazon
Barnes and Noble
Books a Million

Good Health and Long life: Another Perspective

by Rich Kanyali

Paperback
ISBN: 978-1642044201

In Good Health & Long Life—Another Perspective, Rich writes to give a different perspective on health and long life. Many times, the only focus on health is what we do physically such as what we eat, how we exercise and so forth. However, there is a very much untapped side of health which is even more important than the physical. In this book, Rich explores this side and how we can enhance our health and achieve long life.

All books by Rich Kanyali are available on:

RichKanyali.com
Amazon
Barnes and Noble
Books a Million

King David and Other Kings: Life Lessons for Today

by Rich Kanyali

Paperback

ISBN: 978-1-64370-623-8

eBook is also available

Life is full lessons. We can learn from those that went before us and those that are still with us. Although the life of King David was more like a roller coaster, it's one of the most detailed lives we have in the Holy Scriptures. We see the good and the ugly of his life. He made some wrong decisions and he made some great ones too. Nonetheless, the Word of God says that he was a "Man after God's own heart." One thing Rich does not recommend is always learning by your own experience. Sometimes the best way to learn is from the experience of another. We can learn at David's expense (1 Corinthians 10:1-12).

In this book, *King David and Other Kings*, Rich draws out those lessons we can learn from the life of David before and after he was King, and how to avoid the same pitfalls that he fell into. He goes a little further and throws in a bonus of five other kings such as Jehu, Saul, Jehoshaphat, Manasseh, and Josiah as comparisons and contrasts to King David. You will love what you read, and you will find the application of these truths in your life transformational and impactful as Rich has.

All books by Rich Kanyali are available on:

RichKanyali.com
Amazon
Barnes and Noble
Books a Million

Where is Your Prosperity: Countering a Third World Mentality and Learning to Trust God Wherever You Are

by Rich Kanyali

Paperback

ISBN: 978-1-646060-085-6

E-book also available for this book.

None of us chooses where we are born and while some places are more prosperous than others, how do people in some of these less developed or underdeveloped countries prosper? Do they have to relocate to another country, or can they prosper where they are?

There is a misconception that many people have around the world, especially in developing and third world countries. Many of them do not know or have not been taught to believe and trust God where they are located. Many think that the solution to their financial difficulty lies overseas—not where they are.

In this book, Rich challenges that thought process while he shows the reader how people can prosper anywhere.

All books by Rich Kanyali are available on:

RichKanyali.com
Amazon
Barnes and Noble
Books a Million

Got Questions? Got Answers. Common Questions Asked by Christians and Religious people Every Day. Volume One

by Rich Kanyali

Paperback

ISBN: 978-1-64871-741-3

E-book also available for this book.

Whether Christian or non-Christian, every person has questions. Some questions are simple while others are tougher, but all need to be answered. In this book, author Rich Kanyali uses the word of God to answer questions commonly asked such as: Is the bible the word of God? Is believing or faith alone the ONLY requirement for salvation? Why do bad things happen to good people?

From the time he was a young Christian, Rich had the desire to help answer people's questions–and he still does today. Through writing this book, Rich realized that both asking and answering questions are a huge foundation for learning.

The Lord has answered the questions that Rich has had over the years. He is thrilled to share these answers with others. He believes there is no better source of answers than the word of God. Rich uses an approach that is quite different from many bible teachers. He goes into great depth to equip readers with answers that will transform their lives, and in turn, the lives of others.

All books by Rich Kanyali are available on:

RichKanyali.com
Amazon
Barnes and Noble
Books a Million

www.ingramcontent.com/pod-product-compliance
Lightning Source LLC
Chambersburg PA
CBHW070424010526
44118CB00014B/1894